The Concept of Nature

The Concept of Nature

The Herbert Spencer Lectures

Edited by

JOHN TORRANCE
Fellow of Hertford College, Oxford

CLARENDON PRESS · 1992

Oxford University Press, Walton Street, Oxford OX2 6DP
Oxford New York Toronto
Delhi Bombay Calcutta Madras Karachi
Kuala Lumpur Singapore Hong Kong Tokyo
Nairobi Dar es Salaam Cape Town
Melbourne Auckland Madrid
and associated companies in
Berlin Ibadan

Oxford is a trade mark of Oxford University Press

Published in the United States
by Oxford University Press Inc., New York

A catalogue record for this book is available from the British Library

Library of Congress Cataloging in Publication Data
The concept of nature / edited by John Torrance.
(The Herbert Spencer lectures)
Includes bibliographical references.
1. Philosophy of nature–History. 2. Nature. I. Torrance, John.
II. Series.
BD581.C665 1992 210–dc20 92–18125
ISBN 0–19–852276–2

Typeset by Footnote Graphics, Warminster, Wiltshire
Printed in Great Britain by
Biddles Ltd, Guildford and King's Lynn

Preface

The contributions to this volume are based on the Herbert Spencer lectures given at Oxford in 1989. If justification were needed for devoting a set of lectures given in memory of Herbert Spencer to the history of science, one could point to Spencer's own essay *On the Genesis of Science*. Here was the first attempt at an evolutionary theory of scientific progress, a project that has been revived in our own century. However, our contributors do not take a theoretical approach. Instead, three historians of science, a philosopher, a mathematician, and a biologist were invited to describe six significant phases in the history of the concept of nature. Or concept*s*, for a theme that emerges immediately is the diversity of concepts of nature.

Professor Geoffrey Lloyd, discussing the invention of 'nature' by the Greeks, shows how different ideas of nature arose in different polemical contexts. Hippocratic medical writers first claimed that all diseases are natural in controversies with their professional rivals, the purveyors of religious and magical remedies. Among philosophers, the great issue was the relation of nature to convention or law, which produced differing concepts of nature embedded in disputes between teleologists and their opponents. Yet there was an enduring legacy, including the ideas that humans are part of the animal kingdom, and that the causes of phenomena are open to investigation.

That the Middle Ages also lacked a single concept of nature is taken as an axiom by Alexander Murray. He shows how medieval conceptions of the external world were divided in three different ways. Vertically, the learned outlook was far removed from the primitive mentality of the peasantry. But the learned outlook itself contained horizontal divisions, some inherited from antiquity, others due to Neoplatonic and mathematical ideas transmitted by the Arabs. The third division, between what was consistent and inconsistent with the Bible, cut diagonally across both sorts of division. Platonism was in partial conflict with other-worldly

Christianity, Aristotelianism in incomplete agreement with Christianity's view of this world.

The essence of the scientific revolution of the seventeenth century, argues Professor Richard Westfall, was another, quite new conception of nature. Nature was now quantified for the first time: measurement became indispensable for scientific description, as in van Leeuwenhoek's discovery of microscopic life-forms, and for scientific experiment, as with Newton's theory of gravity. Under the influence of Descartes, nature was mechanized, reduced to particles of matter in motion. Thus it was also dehumanized, distanced from the world of sense and common sense, while its scale was extended far beyond the human range by the microscope and telescope. Last but not least, the study of nature was secularized: Newton's natural theology showed that Scripture no longer decided what was true in science; rather, science began to judge what was true in Scripture.

By the nineteenth century John Stuart Mill could say with confidence that 'The word Nature has two principal meanings: it either denotes the entire system of things, with the aggregate of all their properties, or it denotes things as they would be, apart from human intervention.' In the second sense, nature contrasts with artifice, and Mill (like Spencer) attacked the natural theologians' view that nature, in the first sense, is itself an artefact created for man's benefit. While philosophers skirmished, science undermined, and Professor Elliott Sober examines Darwin's contribution to the downfall of teleology.

Darwin's two fundamental hypotheses—'the tree of life', which unites all organisms by common descent, and 'natural selection', which explains speciation by differential environmental selection —are not logically incompatible with theism. But they undercut the plausibility of the argument from design in organic nature, which was one of the natural theologians' favourite defences. Darwin explained adaptation by survival benefit to the organism, not by the good to mankind. Any benefit to mankind is fortuitous; indeed, man himself is, from an evolutionary point of view, a fortuitous product. Moreover, though natural selection improves, it does not perfect. Unlike a beneficent deity, an environment selects only the fittest of the inherited traits it happens to contain, not the fittest conceivable. Finally, Darwin's explanation of species in terms of variation, by taking the differences rather than the similarities of individuals as the point of departure, introduced statistical thinking into biology in place of Aristotelian essentialism.

The last two lectures describe nature as seen by modern science. Professor Roger Penrose claims that the modern physicist's view of nature is constructed from nine theories which, in range and accuracy, qualify for his accolade of SUPERB. His criteria are stringent: no theory outside physics, not even neo-Darwinism, meets them. Newtonian dynamics, with its classical predecessors Euclidean geometry and Archimedean statics, account for three of the nine, to which the nineteenth century added Maxwellian electrodynamics. But electromagnetism was inconsistent with Newton's dynamics, in that they satisfied different relativity principles, and it was the resolution of this inconsistency by Lorentz, Poincaré, and Einstein that began the twentieth-century revolution in physics and supplied two more SUPERB theories, special and general relativity.

The second law of thermodynamics, asserting that entropy in a closed system increases with time, is also, Professor Penrose argues, SUPERB in enabling physicists to understand the macroscopic behaviour of our time-asymmetrical universe. At the other extreme, quantum mechanics combines, in a manner that is still baffling, SUPERB precision at the quantum level with absurdity when applied at the level of classical physics. Finally, Professor Penrose shows how applying the procedures of quantum mechanics to electrodynamics has produced a SUPERB quantum field theory, enabling the minute magnetic charge of an electron to be calculated with experimentally confirmed precision.

The problems which Professor Penrose surmounts in making these theories intelligible to non-scientists demonstrate how modern physics, like its classical predecessor, has made a double leap away from the everyday world—quantitatively, towards the precise measurement of previously indiscriminable magnitudes, both great and small, and qualitatively, into a reality whose strangeness is not only unimaginable, but also not yet describable in a single set of theoretically coherent terms.

The modern biologist's view of nature is still, in essentials,

Darwin's, which has proved a durable foundation for advances at every level. The greatest single advance, in the opinion of Professor Robert May, has been the unlocking of the genetic code in the 1950s, enabling evolutionary processes to be investigated at the molecular level. This sheds light on fundamental questions, such as whether ours is the only inhabited planet in the universe. It promises major advances in immunology and our understanding of the brain. And for better or worse, it makes possible a biological revolution in human history by means of genetic engineering.

A simple, yet basic and difficult, question about organic nature is how many species are there? This and related questions, such as why numbers of species vary with the size of organisms, constitute another expanding field of recent inquiry. Such questions take on a historical dimension when biologists examine extinction rates, or seek to explain population explosions, including that of man, which has now speeded up unprecedentedly the extinction of other species. Professor May ends with the reminder that 'sadly, our search for comprehension of the origins of, and limits to, species diversity takes place against a time limit, with the clock ticking faster as human populations continue to increase.' The biologist, studying nature in Mill's first sense (which, as the Greeks taught us, includes man), now finds less and less of it 'natural' in Mill's second sense.

This volume will have achieved its purpose if it gives the reader a comprehensive view of how scientific conceptions of the external world have varied and developed, from the time when knowledge of nature and man's place in it had to compete with religious beliefs, to the present, when how men use their knowledge has become a major factor in the survival of the race.

Oxford
June 1992

J.R.T.

Contents

Contributors

Geoffrey E. R. Lloyd is Master of Darwin College, Cambridge, and Professor of Ancient Philosophy and Science at Cambridge University. He is a Fellow of the British Academy and of the Japanese Society for the Promotion of Science, and was awarded the Sarton Medal by the US History of Science Society. He is the author of *Polarity and analogy*, *Aristotle: the growth and structure of his thought*, *Early Greek science*, *Thales to Aristotle*, *Greek science after Aristotle*, *Magic, reason and experience*, *Science, folklore and ideology*, *Science and morality in Greco-Roman antiquity*, *The revolution of wisdom*, *Demystifying mentalities*, and *Methods and problems in Greek science*.

Robert M. May is Royal Society Research Professor in the Department of Zoology at Oxford University and at Imperial College, London, and a Fellow of Merton College, Oxford. He is a Fellow of the Royal Society, and a Foreign Associate of the US National Academy of Sciences. He is the author of *Stability and complexity in model ecosystems*, *Theoretical ecology: principles and applications*, *Population biology of infectious diseases*, *Exploitation of marine communities*, *Perspectives in ecological theory*, and *Infectious diseases of humans: dynamics and control* (with Roy M. Anderson).

Alexander Murray is a Fellow and Praelector of University College, Oxford, University Lecturer in Modern History at Oxford University, and a Fellow of the Royal Historical Society. He is the author of *Reason and society in the Middle Ages*, and of numerous articles, chapters, and lectures on medieval thought and religion. He has served as a Director of Studies at the Maison des Sciences de l'Homme in Paris, and at the time these lectures were given he was Visiting Professor of Medieval History at Harvard University.

Roger Penrose is Rouse Ball Professor of Mathematics at Oxford University and a Fellow of Wadham College, Oxford. He is a

Fellow of the Royal Society. He has been awarded the Royal Medal by the Royal Society, and (with S. W. Hawking) the Eddington Medal by the Royal Academy of Science and the Wolf Foundation Prize for Physics. Besides scientific papers his publications include *Techniques of differential topology in relativity* (with W. Rindler) and *Spinors and space–time*.

Elliott R. Sober is Hans Reichenbach Professor of Philosophy at the University of Wisconsin, Madison. He is the author of *Simplicity*, *The nature of selection: evolutionary theory in philosophical focus*, *Reconstructing the past: parsimony, evolution and inference* (for which he received the Lakatos Award), *Core questions in philosophy*, and *Philosophy of biology*.

Richard S. Westfall is Distinguished Professor Emeritus of the History of Science at Indiana University, Bloomington. He has received the Leo Gershoy Award from the American Historical Association and the Sarton Medal from the History of Science Society. He is the author of *Science and religion in seventeenth century England*, *Force in Newton's physics*, *The construction of modern science*, *Never at rest, a biography of Isaac Newton*, and *Essays on the trial of Galileo*.

1

Greek antiquity: the invention of nature

GEOFFREY E. R. LLOYD
Darwin College, Cambridge

Nothing, one might think, could be more natural or more straightforward than the Greeks' conception of nature. After all, does not our own concept of the contrast between the natural and the supernatural stand in direct descent from the ideas of the Greeks? Do we not, thereby, owe to the Greek conception of nature one of the fundamental principles upon which science is based—the science we think of, so naturally, as *natural* science? Does not the concept of nature encapsulate the condition of the possibility of science, that of the intelligibility of the cosmos?

If we pursue such a line of thought, we might—naturally—be led to expect that most of what there is to be said about the Greek conception of nature would consist of an extended testimonial to our indebtedness, a pious rehearsal of what we like to call our legacy. Surely there is not much *new* to be said on that topic—to which I must say immediately that I am very conscious that a vast amount has indeed already been said on it.

But maybe not everything, and maybe not what needs saying on the subject today. For despite the undeniable fact that we are indeed indebted to our Greek past, the line of thinking that I have just sketched out is seriously flawed. Two elementary points will serve as a first indication of this. First it is not as if there ever were *the* Greek concept of nature, by which I mean just the one. To talk of such is to bracket the enormous differences between one philosophical position and another, and between philosophy and what passed as common opinions, as also the divergences between one period and another. It is to talk as if we could blithely generalize over Homer and Proclus, or even over Plato and Aristotle: and that is before we begin to pay attention to the chorus of voices of those who—then as now—invoked the natural to contrast it with the deviant, to justify their own particular attitudes, beliefs, and behaviour, including, not least, their prejudices on gender difference and on sexual practices, where what passes for natural to insiders appears to outsiders as all too obviously culturally determined. What a writer such as Artemidorus tells us about what some Greeks thought *natural* sexual intercourse, is enough to jolt one out of any unreflecting assumption that the Greeks were very much like us—though that is not the subject I shall concentrate on here.

Secondly, if we approach the Greek material not through our term nature, but through their term *phusis* and their term for its study, namely *phusikē*, it soon becomes evident just how strained it is to assimilate what they did under that rubric with what we now think of as physics. If we turn to the treatise called the *Physics* of Aristotle in the expectation of finding anything *we* would recognize as physics, or even anything we would immediately recognize as the ancestor of our physics, we shall be disappointed. Instead of dealing with fundamental particles, or even with matter and energy, Aristotle devotes much of his time to problems to do with causation, time, infinity, continuity. *They* seem to *us* to belong not to physics but to metaphysics and philosophy of science—and to understand how that came about poses quite a challenge, though again that is not one that I can take up here.

So my principal task is to try to recover some of the original, and at points quite alien, complexities of the subject of Greek view*s* (in the plural) about nature. Let me begin, nevertheless, with what may seem some of the more familiar aspects. Let us begin with some of that natural science, though we shall have to move—for the second part of our discussion—from science to politics, and then, in a third, from politics back to some fundamental questions in metaphysics and philosophy of science. 'Scientific, political, speculative', it will be recalled, was how Spencer categorized one of his collections of essays. That suits me very well, for certainly a study of Greek views of nature must span all three. My aim throughout will be not just to report some ancient Greek thoughts, but to focus more particularly on the contexts of their thinking. We must consider not just what they said, but why they said it (insofar as that can be recovered). Whom were they trying to persuade, and what grounds had they to hope to be successful in their persuasion: what were their explicit arguments and how far did they rely on implicit assumptions?

So I turn first to some of that seemingly familiar natural science, and the first point that needs stressing—to *de*familiarize ourselves with this material—is that there was nothing intrinsic in the Greek conception of the *naturalness* of natural phenomena. On the contrary, that idea had to be *invented*, and the most important factor of which we can be sure concerning the circumstances of its invention is the *context of polemic* that surrounded it. Let me elaborate those two points briefly at this stage.

That the idea required invention can be seen most easily by reflecting on its absence from the earliest Greek writings that we have. True, the term *phusis* occurs in a famous passage in the *Odyssey* (X 302ff) where Hermes shows Odysseus a plant, though whether the primary sense here is nature/character or more simply growth is disputed. But to have the idea of the nature of some particular object is not to have the general conception of a *domain of nature* encompassing all natural phenomena. Besides, the plant in question in the *Odyssey* is a *magic* one, *mōly*. Of course no one should expect Homer or Hesiod to discourse on natural science. But it is not just that they do not have occasion to deliver lectures on physics: that would be merely a matter of what they *omit* to say. It is rather what they actually *do* say that is indicative. They are, after all, very free in referring to what *we* might take to be cases of the suspension of the normal regularities of nature. This is high literature, to be sure, and Circe's turning Odysseus's companions into pigs has a symbolic appropriateness that transcends the difficulties that the literal-minded may feel when they ask the question of how precisely she did it: what kind of alchemy was this? Again Hesiod's *Theogony* populates the world with a wild array of hundred-armed creatures, fifty-headed dogs, Chimaeras, Hydras, and the like, which belong to no zoological menagerie but to the no doubt equally vivid representations of the world of the imagination.

We should certainly not imagine that Homer and Hesiod and the audience for whom they composed were somehow unaware of the regularities of what we call natural phenomena. It did not take Aristotle to point out that a human begets a human. It is just inconceivable that Hesiod's contemporaries (or anyone else) were somehow in two minds about the need to sow seed if they wanted corn, even though many no doubt believed that the success of the crop depended also on Zeus, and even though it was only sensible—Hesiod thought—to follow the advice he offered not just on when to plough or shear the sheep, but also about how to avoid the anger of the gods. In that sense some notion that corresponds to nature is assumed—I dare say—universally. But there is all the difference in the world between an implicit assumption and the *explicit* concept.

Nor, once explicit concepts begin to be elaborated in this field, is there any inevitability that the phenomena will come to be grouped in such a way as to make the concept of *nature* central. It so happens that there are certain similarities between our own ideas of nature and some ancient Greek notions of *phusis*: and that is no mere coincidence, of course, but reflects more or less determinate historical influences. However, a glance at the very different but also very sophisticated concepts developed by the ancient Chinese, for example—where *we* will tend to interpret them as referring to what *we* call nature—will serve to make the fundamental point. While Joseph Needham in his pioneering explorations of Chinese science in *Science and civilisation in China* has much to say on their ideas concerning nature, no less than six primary concepts as well as several further subsidiary ones are in play in the texts on which he is commenting—where the more literal renderings of the key terms would be more like Heaven or Sky (tian), pattern (li), things (wu), the way (dao), as well as human nature or disposition (xing) and spontaneity (zi ran, literally self so, the term which with the prefix da, great, comes eventually to form the word used in modern Chinese for nature as in natural science).

So we have two contrasts to bear in mind, not just one: the first that between making certain assumptions concerning certain regularities and having an explicit concept or concepts, and the second within the concepts used in mapping those regularities. The people who were chiefly responsible for explicitly developing some of the characteristically Greek ideas about *phusis* as a domain of nature were the natural philosophers as they were called (*phusikoi*) and the early medical writers. The philosophers usually take pride of place in the discussion of this development, and certainly the earliest of them, Thales in the early sixth century BC, Anaximander and Anaximenes somewhat later, antedate the earliest medical texts we have. But while we have plenty of secondary evidence in the so-called doxographers that suggests that the early natural philosophers went in for naturalistic explanations of natural phenomena in a big way, there are well known difficulties in evaluating this material. We do not even know how far this emphasis reflects the interests of the natural philosophers themselves, or how far it merely represents those of the doxographers—and the need *they* experienced to have *some* theory they could attribute to each early thinker on the various items that were later treated as standard examples of problematic phenomena requiring explanation. As it is, we are presented with a bewildering list of theories, fifteen or so different explanations of lightning and thunder, eleven of earthquakes, twelve of comets and shooting stars, but we are generally *not* given the grounds for them nor the contexts in which they were proposed.

That is true also of one of the few early cases where we can be fairly sure that what we have is the words of the philosopher himself, not a reformulation of them. This is the excerpt from one of Xenophanes' poems we are given by a scholiast to Homer, to the effect that 'she whom men call Iris also is a cloud, purple and red and yellow to behold'. Now that does not seem a particularly inspired suggestion, even if we make allowances for Xenophanes as a very early debutant natural scientist: it is not even as if a rainbow obviously resembles a cloud. But it may be that the thrust of Xenophanes' point (and of other such ideas attributed to other early philosophers) is not so much what is said as what is implicitly denied. Iris—the message is—is no messenger of the Gods, no omen for the future: even though we should beware of assuming that every time some Greek before Xenophanes saw a rainbow they automatically thought of it as a portent.

Yet if that *may have* been the thrust of Xenophanes' point, that is just conjecture on our part. Yet there is no need to guess when it comes to the medical writers' similar ideas and explanations, for there we are dealing with whole original texts and they provide us with all the evidence we need to evaluate not just the basis for the explanations proposed, but also the contexts and the motivations for their proposal. We can give some answers to the questions I said we should bear in mind, of whom they were trying to persuade, and why, and what the grounds were on which they hoped to be persuasive. One *principal* context in which nature comes to be invoked in the medical writers is in relation to the claim that *all* diseases are natural. Against those who maintained or assumed either that particular types of disease are sacred, or that particular incidences of diseases are signs of the gods' displeasure (as when Apollo sends the plague on the Achaeans in the first book of the *Iliad*), some of the Hippocratic writers flatly denied that gods or demons had anything to do with diseases or with their cures.

The best known example is the treatise called *On the sacred disease* which is entirely devoted to the claim that that disease, epilepsy, is natural. There are many interesting details to this writer's arguments that I have discussed at length elsewhere, but I shall concentrate here on the strategy of his attack. It is nonsense, he suggests, to claim that epilepsy is caused by the gods, for every kind of disease has its own nature, *phusis*, and its own cause, *prophasis*. Epilepsy is no exception and the writer offers his own naturalistic account of what causes epileptic fits: I shall come back to that. Actually it is positively impious to think of the gods causing diseases. Moreover, it is not just that this is nonsense—a mistaken inference, he suggests, from the startling character of epileptic attacks. There is more to it than that. The people who go around claiming that it *is* a sacred disease, that they can diagnose which deity is responsible for which variety, and that they can administer the appropriate ritual purification for each, are charlatans and quacks who are in it for the money and who exploit the gullibility of the public.

The obvious but important point about this evidence is that we are dealing with no merely intellectual debate, no mere abstract, theoretical discussion about the nature of nature. On the contrary, this text gives us one side of a bitter controversy between rival traditions of medicine. This is not just a matter of Hippocratic rationalists on the one hand, purifiers on the other. The situation is far more complex than that. To start with, the Hippocratic authors may all invoke natural causes, but they otherwise disagree among themselves fundamentally not just on questions of pathology and treatment, but also on the issue of the status and methodology of the art of medicine itself. On the traditionalist side of the debate, there was not just one strand of religious medicine, but more, and less, established kinds, ranging from the medicine practised in the shrines of Asclepius, all the way to the itinerant sellers of charms and incantations who are the main, and softer, target of *On the sacred disease*.

The fundamental point is that *no* ancient healer could justify his or her right to practice with an appeal to legally recognized qualifications. There were no teaching hospitals; there were no hospitals. There was nothing remotely equivalent to the hallowed initials, MD, FRCP. In classical antiquity, in Greece, there were not even any legal sanctions that could be invoked against medical practitioners of any kind (though the situation changed in this regard in the Roman empire). But this means that every style of healing competed on equal terms with every other (and temple medicine, we know, was as popular as any). It is all very well our Hippocratic author remarking that the purifiers were in it for the money: he was himself. We know, then, whom this and other Hippocratic authors were trying to persuade: they include clients and potential pupils as much as anyone who might be interested in joining a theoretical—philosophical or scientific—debate.

We can, too, evaluate the grounds and justification for his counter-claims to the claims the purifiers made. His explanation of the sacred disease is that it is caused by the blocking of the veins in the brain, which he says happens especially to the phlegmatic—the bilious are less affected. That last point gives him an additional argument that it was nothing to do with gods, for they would not discriminate thus between phlegmatic and bilious constitutions. But this explanation of epilepsy is, of course, quite fanciful. Worse, so too are the anatomical theories with which he backs it up, his equally imaginary account of the blood-vessels in the body—I shall spare you the details. Worse still, he appears to claim, against the purifiers, that he has the right technique to effect a cure—of epilepsy as of most other diseases. This turns out to be a matter of controlling the temperature and humidity of the body by regimen (food and exercise), and this too, so far as epilepsy is concerned, must be considered pie in the sky.

Nature was, no doubt, invoked by medical writers and natural philosophers on some occasions when something like a plausible explanatory theory was available. Eclipses would be a case in point. But, as my example shows, on many others it was a mere act of faith—we might even say bluff—to claim to be able to understand, let alone to control, the phenomena in question.

My argument thus far is that some of those who insisted on the category of the natural used it to demarcate and justify their style of inquiry, their methodology, in contrast to those of rivals whom they were hoping to put out of business. We cannot be sure that Xenophanes had it in for diviners (though he certainly criticizes on several grounds a number of prestigious professions which were rival claimants to excellence). But some Hippocratic authors used nature to rule out any possibility of any *super*natural interference in diseases. The concept of the natural had its attractions for them precisely because it enabled a wedge to be driven between *their* medical practice and that of the competition. Their rivals, the Hippocratics would claim, make an elementary category mistake. All diseases are natural phenomena, each has its nature, its own causes, its own natural explanation. However, the grounds those same Hippocratic writers themselves used to justify their own positive claims to have understood those causes were often tenuous or non-existent.

Again if one may interject a Chinese comparison and contrast to point up features of the Greek experience, there were Chinese too who were as critical as any Greeks of certain traditional Chinese beliefs and practices that they considered to be groundless or based on superstitious fears. But they did not attempt to defeat whole classes of opponents by invoking a category of the natural that ruled out what is contrary to nature. Rather they dealt with error, folly, superstition, as they encountered them—by exposing their consequences, for example—without recourse to some general categorial principle concerning the natures of things which was supposed to secure a firm distinction between the investigable and the superstitious—except that the Greeks' expressed confidence that everything had its nature and its causes generally lived uneasily with a fundamentally shaky grasp of what these actually were.

But to those criticisms of mine of the Hippocratics a counter might be offered that might go like this. Maybe the Hippocratic theorists could not explain all or even many diseases, and could not cure them either, and maybe most of the pre-Socratic natural philosophers were all at sea in their explanations of rainbows and comets and earthquakes. That point might be conceded. But, the counter might be, at least their explanations were of the *right type*. Eventually more and better explanations would be given: but they would share the essential characteristic of the earliest hesitant attempts, namely that they appealed purely to natural factors. So if the expression of what *could* be explained *then was* an act of faith (even with an element of bluff thrown in), it was a *legitimate* act of faith—in the *promise* of delivery of the new style of wisdom, even if that new style had not *actually* delivered much at the time the original faith was expressed.

That counter has some force, but its main weakness is obvious. It was not as if the justification could reasonably take the form that the act of faith was legitimate because the way ahead—for science—was clear, in the sense that the path to follow was. It could not take that form for the simple reason that—except perhaps in the broadest possible terms—the path that science *should* follow was anything but agreed. Even those who shared a view of the importance and desirability of the goal of understanding nature, were locked in bitter dispute over what would constitute such understanding—and accordingly also over how to set about securing it. I shall have more to say on this at the end.

More immediately, the invocation of the category of the natural in such a manner as we have seen in the early philosophers and medical writers depends, for its plausibility, on having a reasonably clear answer to the question of what that category included. At first sight the answer may seem simple: the answer must be everything, where 'everything' ranges over all material objects, their properties and characteristics. But three problems immediately present themselves of varying degrees of difficulty, the first to do with exceptions to the rule, the second to do with human nature, and the third to do with the contrast between nature and culture (or as the Greeks said *phusis* and *nomos*)—where the last two will take us into the second main section of our inquiry, into politics.

As for exceptions to the rule—my first difficulty—the point for the moment is straightforward and we can be brief. As Aristotle insisted, what is natural comprises what is true always or for the most part. An explanation, to be an explanation, must bring the particular explanandum in question under a general law and Aristotle will see proper explanations as making reference to the formal cause, the essence, the nature of the object or event investigated. But if that does splendidly for the regularities of nature—when a human being begets a human being—what about breaches to those regularities, monsters, sports? They had, of course, quite often been grist to the mill of those who saw the hands of the divine or demonic at work in the world—so the natural philosophers had better have *some* account that they could offer on this type of question. Aristotle's first stage answer is to insist on a distinction. 'According to nature', *kata phusin*, in one sense picks out the regularities, the law-like—where the contrast is with what is contrary to nature, *para phusin*, in the sense of an exception to the rule. But the exceptions are still not *super*natural—not *para phusin* in that other sense—for they arise, for example, from the chance intersection of two or more causal chains each of which is a perfectly good example of some regularity. Chance is just the name for such an intersection and there is no more to it than that. Nature evinces regularities and that is what entitles us to speak of the essential characteristics of things as their natures: but those regularities are not exceptionless, even if the exceptions themselves do not *stand outside* the domain of nature (for nothing does that). There will be more to say about other aspects of this problem later, but as a first stage answer it may suffice for now.

But that problem is nothing like so severe as those that arise in connection with the issue of *human* nature. It was, perhaps, one of the strengths of the pagan Greek view of humans that there was no question of human beings *not* being part of nature. Humans are living creatures, *zōia*, and clearly belong to the same genus as all other animals. Where other cultures and religions may so stress the *gap* between humans and animals that 'animals' do not include 'humans', the pre-Christian Greeks generally assumed co-membership in a common genus.

One asymmetry was, however, quite widespread. The animal series was often used as a template to apprehend and describe the differences between human characters. This was not a formally elaborated part of any natural philosopher's theory, but rather a common and deeply ingrained way of thinking and talking about the world. One of the ways animals were 'good to think with' was as providing a set of models for human characters—the fox for cunning, the lion for courage, the boar for steadfastness, the deer for timidity and so on. But one feature of this way of thinking and talking that stands out is that, on the animal side, it is distinct species and genera that provide the markers, while on the human side, what is thus marked is character types *within* the *one* (human) species. That tends to stress and enlarge the differences, to suggest more permanent character traits in humans than would otherwise be assumed—as if Ajax were *always* like a wild boar. That is partly *why* the animal series is so used (and was so used not just by the ancient Greeks, of course), but we should be clear that that use is not neutral, nor entirely innocent, in its implications for our understanding of human behaviour. No doubt to make sense of one another's behaviour we need to assume some more or less stable character traits. Yet with some uses of animal comparisons it is not just stability, but fixity or even unmodifiability that is assumed: for the leopard cannot change his spots.

Nor is it just human character traits that were sometimes thus type-cast. Another context in which the Greeks favoured a strong differentiation within humans is that of their physical constitutions. Indeed this notion interacts with the differentiation of human characters in the context of theories of the humours. The phlegmatic, the bilious, the sanguine, the melancholic man or woman were assumed to possess not just stable character dispositions, but also (as it were) different biochemistries. To be sure, that is mainly a development of the post-classical period. But differentiation between the physical constitutions of different groups already figures in the fifth century BC, in such classic discussions as that of the different natures, *phusies*, of the Egyptians, Libyans, Scythians, Greeks, and others in the Hippocratic treatise *On airs waters places*. As that writer puts it (ch. 13) there are human natures that are like wooded, well-watered mountains, others like light dry land, others like marshy meadows, others like a bare parched earth. This writer happens to believe that everything grows to a greater size and beauty in Asia (ch. 12), even though the Greeks have superior characters. But the potentially ominous racialist implications of the type of thesis he advances are obvious, even though, let me repeat, whatever their sense of their own superiority to Barbarians and to slaves, and their readiness to deploy a rich vocabulary of abuse for those—including other Greeks—unlike themselves, the ancient Greeks generally were clear that inferior humans too are still members of the same, human, species.

The writer of that Hippocratic treatise holds that while human physique is largely determined by ecology, human character depends in part on another factor. What, I asked earlier, was to be included under *phusis*, nature? I first answered everything, all material objects—and that was the answer the natural philosophers needed in order to squeeze out the category of the *super*-natural. But of course in the sphere of human behaviour *phusis* was regularly opposed to its standard antonym, *nomos*, covering customs and conventions as well as laws. It is this factor that *On airs waters places* appeals to in order to explain how it is that members of the same *genos* or race, brought up in the same ecological conditions, may nevertheless behave quite differently. This happens, he says, when they *live under different political systems*. As clear evidence for this (a *mega tekmērion*) he cites the fact that where the inhabitants of Asia are *not* ruled by tyrants, they are the most warlike of peoples (ch. 16), even though bravery is not, by nature, part of their character (cf ch. 24).

Yet as is well known, just how the antithesis between nature and convention was to be taken was itself enormously controversial in antiquity, a topic on which many a modern book and article have been written. From one point of view that contrast was crucial as the chief means of securing what (on *that* view) the domain of science is to include. For one type of aspiring natural scientist 'nature' encompasses what holds of natural phenomena, including of humans as the animals they are, while 'custom' stands for society-specific modes of behaviour. Broadly, *phusis* falls to science, *nomos* to sociology or political philosophy. Yet that was far from being the only point of view expressed, either on where the dividing line between the two came, or on the moral and political connotations and implications of the two terms.

For some, *nomos* was *mere* custom and convention, the rules and regulations that a person with the power to do so will ignore—or manipulate to their own advantage. Social codes in all their variety, Callicles says in Plato's *Gorgias* (492c), are a nonsense, *phluaria*: they are set up by the weak (483bc) but according to nature it is *just* for the stronger to have more than the weak. Thrasymachus in the *Republic* (338e) takes a different line on the origins of laws, when he puts it that each interest group, once it gets into power, fixes them to suit their own advantage. But while there are different developments and formulations of the point in yet other texts in Plato (in his account of the atheists in *Laws* X, for instance), in Thucydides (the Melian debate, V 85ff), and in the sophist Antiphon, a common theme found in many variations is that the only universally valid principle is that might is right.

But against that group of positions there were those who adopted a more positive evaluation of *nomos* in the sense of law, as the guarantor of justice and, precisely, what marks humans out from other animals. Justice and shame, the sophist Protagoras is made to say in Plato (*Protagoras* 322c), are given to all humans, and it is they that provide the basis for civilized social life. And there are others again who resist too sharp a contrast between the two terms, not least Plato himself, who sees the same demiurgic intelligence at work in *nature* as should be present also in the ideal human *law*-giver.

No agreement obtained, therefore, either on whether *both* nature and law are charged with moral significance, or on that significance, if they are. While for some, we said, nature is *not* the domain of moral or evaluative judgements, for many others it was, even though how they cashed that out varied all the way from the view that might is right to the notion that there are, in some sense, unwritten laws of nature—moral laws, that is. The whole controversy is, of course, often associated with the challenge to traditional moral values for which those favourite bogeymen of Plato, the sophists, are often held to be primarily responsible. But whatever the degree of their involvement, let alone responsibility, it would clearly be wrong to assume that this was *just* a sophistic controversy, as the continuation of some themes in Aristotle amply shows. It is time now to explore his contribution to the issues in some detail.

Aristotle takes as firm a line as any on the investigability of nature—the topic we began with. We have seen that he *dis*allows the *super*natural with an insistence on the distinction between it and what is merely an exception to a general rule: the former is not, the latter is, countenanced. He gives us, too, a definition of nature as what has an inner source of movement and rest, and he sets out with great lucidity the task of the natural philosopher in giving causal explanations of four types, formal, final, efficient, material. The way in which the concept of nature is deployed in the heart of his political philosophy is, then, all the more striking. For there, as is so well known, humans are defined as by *nature* political animals, more strictly as animals that live in city-states. Moreover, in a further notorious section of *Politics* book I, slavery is defended as a *natural* institution. Again even certain types of economic exchange—those that do not involve wealth-getting for its own sake—are said to be natural. It is not that Aristotle ignores the differences between moral and political philosophy on the one hand, physics and natural philosophy on the other. On the contrary, he points them out repeatedly. Thus the sphere of *moral* excellence is quite distinct from that of merely natural excellence, for moral excellence depends on (moral) choice, *proairesis*, which only adult humans possess, not the other animals and not even children. Yet there are these in no sense merely figurative appeals to nature in his political philosophy.

Coming to terms with this at first sight quite alien feature of his thought is no easy task: but there are arguments to evaluate as well as deep-seated assumptions, not to say prejudices, with which to grapple. That humans are political animals (to use that conventional translation) is arrived at not as a result of some piece of Academic scholastic definition-mongering of the type that gave us the shattering insight that man is a rational two-legged animal. Rather it is the conclusion of a piece of analytic reasoning. The argument takes an evolutionary form, though Aristotle is not committed to all the evolutionary aspects of the hypothesis. All animals naturally desire to reproduce. Like other animals, male and female humans naturally form associations for reproductive purposes: so that the basic mode of association, the household (*oikia*) is (as we might put it) founded on biological needs. But the household is not self-sufficient: to fulfil more than their daily, ephemeral, needs several households agglomerate first into villages, then into more complete or perfect associations, a process that culminates in the *polis*, the city-state, which, we are told, *came to be* for the sake of life, but *is* for the sake of the good life. So the *polis* is by nature, *phusei*, given that the first associations are: for *it* is *their* end, *telos*, and nature is an end. Whatever we may think about where the argument ends, some modern commentators would agree at least to its beginning, to the proposition that humans are social animals with a minimum size for a viable human community.

His argument concerning slavery shares some of the same features. He is well aware of an alternative view, the idea that it is merely by convention. *nomōi*, that slaves are slaves, and that naturally, *phusei*, there is no distinction between slave and free. Evidently when the naturalness of what he *claims* to be natural had been flatly denied, he has that much more of an obligation to *show* its naturalness, and he concedes to the opposition straight away that some do become enslaved unjustly and are slaves merely by convention or law. However, that does not lead him to make any concessions at all as to the general principle, that the distinction between master and slave *is* natural, a principle he supports, first, by citing a battery of proportional analogies. Master is to slave as soul is to body, or as old is to young, or as male to female. Yet (as so often) the argument is not merely one by analogy, for all those paired relationships exemplify the generic distinction to be found (he says) in every composite whole constituted of parts, namely that between what rules and what is ruled.

Here too then the determination of what is natural involves a biological and sociobiological dimension, but the way the sociobiological data at Aristotle's command are put to work is remarkable. He can, to be sure, claim that the distinction between soul and body is to be found in all living creatures, for 'soul' just picks out what makes the living creature the *living* thing it is. But as for his representation of the relationship between males and females, Aristotle the zoologist knows very well that there are plenty of species of animals where the females are stronger, bigger, more dominant, and longer lived than the males, and some too (such as the bear and panther) where they are more courageous. If we add up the exceptions that Aristotle allows to the rule that males are longer lived than females, they amount to a considerable list, one that includes most of the ovipara and larvipara. Yet that does not stop him from reiterating that naturally, *phusei*, males are longer lived than females.

There is a recurrent move here, in both arguments, that relates to a fundamental tension in Aristotle's conception of nature. On the one hand the natural is equated with what is true always or for the most part. On the other, what is natural is the goal, the end, the ideal. Thus it is *better*, Aristotle claims, for right to be differentiated from left, and again male from female, and again master from slave. But the first of each of those pairs is the *telos* or end, the second *for the sake of* that end. From the point of view of what just is the case, females are as *regular* as males, of course. But from the point of view of their function or capacity, they are, he says, like natural deformities, natural (no doubt) because regular, but deformities because Aristotle is convinced that they are to be defined by an *in*capacity, the incapacity to concoct the blood into semen (i.e. in the way males do). From the point of view of regularities he might just as well have defined males by *their* incapacity to produce menses and to give birth: but Aristotle would not dream of doing so.

The nature of the species is, then, captured by the mature—male—specimen. But nature is a goal not just in an intraspecific perspective, but also in certain interspecific ones (though this is more controversial). Throughout Aristotle's zoology the human species is the yardstick by which other animals are measured. Anomalies such as species where the females are longer lived do not shake his belief—cannot shake his belief—that *naturally* (now in the sense of the ideal) the male is longer lived—for that is true, he believes (and it was true in his day), of humans. Similarly it is better for right (the side from which movement begins) to be differentiated from left: but when he encounters animals with no strong differentiation between the two sides, that is a mark of their inferiority. Again he defines upper as the direction from which food is taken in—and accepts the consequence that plants, fed from their roots, are upside down. In humans alone, indeed, the upper parts are directed towards the upper part of the universe. In humans *alone*, he is prepared to say (*de Partibus Animalium* 656a10ff), the *natural* parts are *according to* nature. What is normal or natural in the animal kingdom is evidently no matter, here, of counting heads or species, but is arrived at by reflection on the principles instantiated in the animals assumed to be *superior*, or more particularly in the species assumed to be supreme, namely humans.

The application of similar ideas in the *Politics* is particularly blatant. Humans are the *only* species of animals in which the distinction between master and slave is found. They are the only *polis*-forming animals, too, though other species are gregarious and are described as political, *politika*, in the loose or general sense of *social* animals. But these unique features of human beings do not cause Aristotle to hesitate to attach the characteristic 'natural' to them—rather than treating them as belonging to the *nomos*, law, convention, culture, side of the dichotomy. The uniqueness of the features in question does not deter him because what is natural is here equated with the ideal. The truly natural specimen is the animal in its prime. The truly natural species, the species that is most in accord with nature as what is capable of fulfilling the most potentialities for the good life, is the human species.

There is, of course, much more to Aristotle's political arguments than I can indicate here, including much of his analysis for which no claim as to the naturalness of human social institutions is entered. But I hope to have said enough to bring out one fundamental feature of his use of the concept of nature, and not just in politics, namely that while it may often appear merely descriptive (where it corresponds to what is just usually the case) it is also and just as frequently profoundly normative. We should be clear that there is nothing covert about this. It is not that Aristotle slips unwittingly into some crass confusion. On the contrary, it is an explicit and avowed part of Aristotle's whole programme of inquiry in *every* area of thought that explanations should be teleological in character and include reference to the good, where this is appropriate. It is true that he explicitly *denies*, in his zoology, that *everything* (without exception) has a final cause, that is that all the parts of animals serve some end. Some parts are as they are *not* because they serve some good directly, but merely because they are the by-products of other processes (though *they* do). He specifies the gall-bladder as an example, the end-product of the processes of digestion, and if they certainly serve an obvious good—the survival of the creature no less—not all their residues do. However, the natural philosopher can, and Aristotle insists should, consider the goods that objects and events serve, and where these are present, they form part of the *explanations* of the objects and events in question. There can be no question of giving a satisfactory account of the blood-vessels, say, if just their structure and constitution are considered. Their function, the good they serve (which Aristotle thinks of in terms of nourishing the body) has to be included also, a principle he applies not just in zoology but throughout his natural science and beyond—notably within his political philosophy as we have seen.

So this takes me now to the third and final subject area I identified at the outset, the metaphysical and philosophical assumptions that underlie the various competing and conflicting Greek conceptions of nature. It was Aristotle's view, and one he shared with Plato, that the natures of things include their goals, the good they fulfil or actualize. On this view, the natural philosopher, we said, must consider and include, indeed *especially* include, teleological explanations. But that was not the only view put forward in classical antiquity. Much to the chagrin of Plato and of Aristotle, there were those who pursued the goal of understanding the world on the basis of the directly opposed, anti-teleological, assumption—namely that the *only* explanations that are to count as explanations are those that relate to the physical (we often say mechanical) interactions of things. The atomists' programme was represented by Plato as atheistical (and by Aristotle sometimes as appealing to mere chance). But on *their own* terms, *they* sought to investigate the necessary causal connections of things.

Nor was this the only fundamental disagreement that separated opposing schools of thought, whether among theorists who agreed at least on the possibility of understanding, or between them and others who denied that very possibility. There were, for instance, radical sceptics for whom it is futile to attempt to comprehend nature. These sceptics were careful not to say that it is *impossible* to comprehend nature, for to *assert* that would be to be as dogmatic as their opponents. Rather *no* assertions as to how nature is, nor about the underlying realities or hidden causes of things, can be made. These radical sceptics content themselves with saying how things appear. The honey appears sweet: but as to its being sweet or not, on that judgement should be suspended.

But even among those who rejected scepticism and maintained the possibility and the value of the investigation of nature, there were disputes that stretch beyond the major quarrel between teleologists and anti-teleologists that I have already referred to. This is yet another vast topic to which I cannot attempt to do justice here. But just two aspects may be noted briefly.

First, on an issue that sees Plato and Aristotle on different sides, there was a question of the admissibility of change and coming-to-be in what is investigable. In Plato's Theory of Forms the range of what is fully knowable does not extend beyond that of unchanging being. Particulars that come to be and are subject to change are then assigned to the realm of opinion as contrasted with that of knowledge. Now Aristotle shares Plato's reservations about the possibility of attaining knowledge of the particular *as the particular it is*: he agrees that understanding is of the universal. But he is clearer as to the investigability of changing objects and more positive on the status of particulars. The regularities that the natural philosopher reveals are the regularities instantiated by physical objects, not (as in some formulations in Plato) merely imitated by them. For Aristotle, as I have already remarked, nature is indeed defined as a *principle* of change. While you and I, natural objects that we are, indeed change, that does not diminish our claim to substancehood: indeed, of course, in the terminology of the *Categories* we are primary substances.

The second debate involves a larger cast of characters but again sees Plato and Aristotle on different sides—on the question of the relations between physics (the study of nature) and mathematics. For a claim to full understanding to be sustained, does it or does it not have to have a mathematical form or be expressible mathematically? For Plato, certainly, mathematics is superior to the study of becoming, though itself inferior to dialectic—and we should not exaggerate the extent to which Plato was clear about a programme of mathematizing physics. But for many practitioners in the exact sciences it was precisely through the mathematization of the phenomena that the underlying regularities were to be revealed. That was the great strength of what we correctly call the mathematical astronomy of antiquity, and of Archimedes' statics and hydrostatics, as also of such other exact, mathematical, sciences as optics and harmonics. Yet for Aristotle the priorities between physics and mathematics are clear. Not for him the view that it is only what is mathematizable that can be fully understood, and if the rest of physics could not be, so much the worse for physics. His position is that the truths that mathematics reveals are truths *about* the physical realities. Mathematics deploys a powerful technique of abstraction, to be sure, but its subject-matter is no separate realm of mathematical entities, but, precisely, the mathematical properties of *physical* objects.

I issued warnings about generalizing about the Greek view of nature and I have put a bewildering variety of ideas before you. But it is time now to take stock. I began by referring to a naïve view that might suppose that the Greek concept of nature is natural. By now you will have some idea of how controversial it was—I mean among the Greeks themselves. My argument has been that the theorists we have been studying did not (so much) discover nature—like Columbus hitting America. Rather they created, they invented, their own distinctive and divergent ideas, often in direct and explicit confrontation with their rivals. The concept was forged in controversy, notably as the underpinning to the claims made by new styles of wisdom in their attempts to outbid more traditional kinds. The paradox was that—as some have said of mythology—the idea of nature was supposed to stand simply for what is there, for what can be taken for granted. Yet what that comprised was repeatedly contested, not just so far as the natural world in general went, but also as far as human nature is concerned. For some the domain of natural science was sharply contrasted with that of human culture, and nature was opposed to art as well as to convention. But for others nature was itself permeated with values, and a resource for moral philosophy, while for yet others it was rather a covert source of moralizing where the category of the natural was used to legitimate a point of view specific to the interests of some particular group.

So if we stand back and ask what the Greeks stood for, the answer must be complex and almost every generalization has to be qualified. One recurrent notion was that of humans as part of nature, humans as members of the animal kingdom, though special members no doubt. Another, of prime importance in one of the leading controversies, was the idea of the investigability of the causal relations of natural phenomena, although that was contested (by the sceptics) and even those who did not contest it disagreed about the character of the understanding that could be attained and the way to set about attaining it. In their enthusiasm for their own investigations, many ancients—as we have seen—promised a good deal more than they could deliver. If eventually there were to be some remarkable deliveries, we should not imagine that the ancients themselves had a clear and uncluttered vision of the way ahead, let alone were unanimous in their views. On the contrary, that was as disputed as many of the solutions to particular problems were. We have almost as many theories of nature as of, say, earthquakes. However, the value of those disputes is not diminished, but may if anything be increased, by the very range of disagreement—since that secured the exploration of the widest possible range of answers to the questions of the proper subject-matter of the study of nature, and the outer limits of its intelligibility.

On that view, one of the most notable products of classical antiquity lies not so much in the actual natural scientific theories proposed, as in the competing theories of nature and of natural science themselves. It would be an exaggeration to say that the sole Greek contribution to science lies in the philosophy of science, but it can be argued that that was one of their more durable contributions.

But the paradoxicality of the situation deserves underlining. Nature was what was presupposed to be there to investigate: its supposed objective reality was what guaranteed the viability of the investigation. Yet what that vaunted objective reality consisted in was contested in every conceivable respect. If nature was invoked as a rallying cry for the new natural science, the investigators, in Greek antiquity, were not exactly *rallied*, and while today no one can doubt the strength of the forces that stand for natural science, it is not that our own more mundane ideas of what is natural have been completely sanitized in the process.

Two last points to conclude. In the early days the bid to give naturalistic explanations of natural phenomena went, one might say, not just with a demystifying of the universe, but with a certain trivializing of it. Poet that he himself was, how could Xenophanes reduce Iris to a cloud? Yet if the advance of what passed for science meant in some cases the exclusion of poetry, we should be careful not to exaggerate the point. There is poetry and there is poetry: there is elevated thought in verse and elevated thought in prose. I would not claim that such verse as most ancient scientists wrote is great poetry. Ptolemy's epigram (referring to his feeling when he does astronomy that his feet no longer touch the earth and it is as if he were feasting with the gods) ranks perhaps not much higher than doggerel. Yet there is no mistaking the thrill the scientists sometimes felt and expressed at the exploration of nature and the discovery of its workings. Aristotle has to defend the study of anatomy against the prejudices of the day. But he does well to quote Heraclitus in that defence: there are gods even here. The point is that one of the chief motivations of science (as again Aristotle remarks in the opening of the *Metaphysics*) was curiosity, the desire to learn, the excitement of discovery, even on occasion a certain wonder at the objects of that investigation.

My second point is the converse of that one. The motivations of the ancient scientist had indeed mainly to be personal and private, and they were often moral, even moralistic, or religious. There was no way in which society was going to support science, there were not even many (though there were some) rich patrons who would do so for the prestige attached. So science existed with a minimum institutional framework, certainly without the complex institutions of education and research we are familiar with, all of which testify to the standing of science in our own culture. But with the standing goes, of course, a certain aggressiveness, in the modern bid to convert knowledge to what are represented as useful purposes, an aggression also sometimes with regard to the means used to get the knowledge, where questionable means are justified on the off chance that some useful ends *might* be served.

Many ancient Greek views of nature were simplistic and on many occasions they were used to bolster dubious conclusions as to the place of human beings in the scheme of things. But the Greeks were not driven to study nature in order to control and appropriate it. To be sure, that may be as much because the possibilities of the exploitation of such knowledge as they had were limited—as for any other reason: for what can you do with a system of astronomical models *but* contemplate them? And Aristotle certainly spoke of plants and other animals being, in some sense, for the sake of humans. Yet that does not mean that *we* have any reasons to be complacent, in our attempts to strike a balance between the notion that nature is just there to be exploited and the reservations that might be held to follow from the recognition of ourselves as part of that nature. Ineluctably modern as we are, we are still in no position to use the criticism and analysis of ancient opinions as any grounds for self-congratulation about our own capacity to reach a steady view on the problems which those opinions addressed, on the possibility of science, on the stability of human character, on the boundaries of nature and culture, and on the proper relationship between ourselves and our environment.

Indeed, for reaching a steady view on those problems it may even be wise to make the most of those ancient opinions and controversies as resources for our own self-criticism and analysis. Certainly one may take a first, salutary, step forwards unmasking the powerful claims to inevitability that often accompany the appeal to nature by following up those ancient controversies and the other indications that point to the circumstances of what I have called its invention.

2

Nature and man in the Middle Ages

ALEXANDER MURRAY
University College, Oxford

Why do the miracles in the Bible not happen now? The answer is, if they were to happen all the time they would stop astonishing us. Let us look about us. See how day and night turn in their perpetual round, and how the sky and stars follow their changeless courses. See how the seasons change, and the leaves grow and wither on the boughs. Look at the unquenchable vitality within seeds, and at the beauty of light, colours and sounds, of smells and of tastes, in all their variety. Now let us go and talk to someone who was seeing this for the first time. Could *he* talk to *us*? He would be struck dumb by all these miracles. Yet we think them ordinary. That is not because we understand them. Their causes remain a deep mystery. No, it is because they are never absent from our experience.

That was written by St. Augustine of Hippo around AD 391, in a book destined to be familiar to western writers for the next thousand years. Some of them would echo its sharp psychology in their own works.[1]

We human beings could not live if we were astonished *all* the time. We have to take some things for granted, like the mechanisms by which I speak and others hear my words. As a species we normally divide everything around us into things that astonish us and things that do not, the latter further dividing into things we do, and things we do not understand. These lines across our experience vary in each of us, and in succeeding societies. Their patterns are complex and belong to what we call the history of ideas, and in particular, in this case, to the history of the idea of nature.

Within this long history I shall be concentrating on the Middle Ages: the period from soon after the death of St. Augustine, in the fifth century, to the fifteenth: a time longer than that which divides us from King Canute, but which seems—whether or not through optical illusions: I will touch on that—to have a certain unity.

So let me start by saying how I shall understand 'nature'. In a magazine-title the word 'nature' does not always tell you what is inside. It may be a discovery in physics, articles on birds and plants, pictures of Scotland, recipes with nuts and raisins in, or other things. A similar variety can be found in works of history. But the meanings broadly divide into those inside, and outside, man: moral, and what we call physical. Of course they all stem from one Idea. Aristotle himself linked the two kinds of meaning—as Professor Lloyd pointed out in the first lecture in the series[2]—and for that reason alone they would be often linked in medieval thought. And perhaps I can add, to Professor Lloyd's perceptive remarks that the story of the idea of nature, in any age, is the visible side of another, invisible history, to which it is antithetical: that of will and intelligence. Nature, both within us and without us, is something that is not *us*. I shall talk later of medieval animism, and come back to this, too.

However unified at source, the various ideas of nature have had slightly different histories, and I have had to choose. We all could have learned something, no doubt, from a lecture on nature in medieval ethics: the good nature that makes unnatural behaviour bad, and the bad nature that needs grace to mend it.[3] If I neglect that, it is mainly through having plenty to talk about without it, together, perhaps, with a suspicion that it would need a venue further from the Department of Zoology, which would not be impartial.

So I shall be talking, not about nature inside man, in ethics, but about nature *out*side man. This too has more than one connotation. Modern historians sometimes say that medieval people could not appreciate the beauty of external nature. Let a medievalist be indignant. Augustine's word about light and colours in that passage was *pulchritudo*. Even if we did not have all that stained glass we would know that many thoughtful medieval people thought natural light and colours beautiful. As for scenery, a famous thirteenth century philosopher numbered among the attractions of his university city, Paris, that its environs had air and rivers fitting for philosophers, the beauty of its fields, meadows and mountains refreshing the eyes of people wearied by study.

A lecture could be given about that, too.[4]

But this paper will be about external nature in another sense, that of what we often call the natural world: the mysterious world around us which even now man has very little control of, and which medieval thinkers of all periods, taking to themselves a Greek word, sometimes called the *machina mundi*: meaning not so much 'machine' as 'device', the ensemble, that is, of everything except us. This is still a big subject. And in choosing which side of it to tackle I have felt, and resisted, three temptations. If, when you hear what the temptations were, you wish I had yielded to one or more of them and think you have been brought here under false pretences, then you can slip away now without offence. So I shall tell you.

The first was to create a montage of views on comets, unicorns and so on, from medieval encyclopaedias, like the *De natura rerum* of Isidore of Seville in the seventh century, or Vincent of Beauvais's *Speculum naturale* in the thirteenth, and many in between. These views can be entertaining, but this task has been well done by others, and one of its troubles here is that many of the views come from much older sources, so are not really medieval. More will be said of that, too, indirectly.

The second temptation was to tackle medieval science, not in any attempt to show that Roger Bacon invented submarines or that this or that thinker was 'ahead of his time', but as a close-up picture of some particular problem, like the one on which our own Alasdair Crombie has written with great originality—and that is itself a reason for my avoiding it—quantification in physics: the beginnings of the reduction of things to mathematics.[5] Actually I shall touch on that too at the end of this lecture, but from the reverse side. The history of science, however, I also rejected, not just through incapacity but because of a suspicion that 'science' is ultimately a modern category rather than medieval, and may distort our enquiry from the start.

The third temptation was the strongest of all. It was to rehearse, in the manner of *haute vulgarisation*, some of the best recent literature on the development of meanings in the *word* nature, especially in the twelfth century. M. C. Chenu, for instance, describes the quickening of interest in nature in twelfth-century Chartres, and at the end of the century in Paris, as shown in the titles and subjects of books; and he chronicles in particular the appearance, after a long but withdrawn prehistory, of an allegorical Natura with a capital 'N', in philosophical poetry. Chenu's study is easily available in English.[6] The background to these developments has meanwhile been explored in depth by Tullio Gregory, in studies only (to my knowledge) in Italian. By scrutiny especially of commentary on Plato. Gregory has thrown light on shifting nuances in the use of the word *natura* in these same milieux. Some scholars, for instance, leaned towards an idea of nature as essentially a power of generation and reproduction—an idea which clearly spills over into the moral aspect of 'nature'; others saw it more as a force within things, producing effects according to regular patterns; yet others, without going all the way to giving it a capital 'N', saw nature as the ensemble of what was called secondary causation, that is, causation other than God.[7]

You will say I have yielded in part to this third temptation, by renouncing it at too great a length. If so, it is with an ulterior purpose. In particular, among many lessons from these two scholars to be among our premisses here, special attention should be drawn to those two 'natures' respectively with big and small 'N': the allegorical figure who—as C. S. Lewis said medieval allegory generally did[7]—helped people conceive an abstraction; and, with the small 'n', the force within things, producing like effects from like causes. In Latin:

vis quaedam rebus insita similia de similibus operans.[9]

There, then, are the three temptations. You may wonder where your vacillating lecturer found force within himself to resist them. The answer lies with the eponym of this series. Writing soon after Darwin, Herbert Spencer was to Darwin as the general to the particular, and sought, with a broad sweep over human society, to identify its principles of evolution. Any scholar, therefore, with even a faint yearning to do the same could not expect a fitter occasion to do so. You may at times think my sweep *too* broad; and in that case I can only quote Spencer's own words when in 1864 his proposed *System of philosophy* was subject to similar critical murmurs.

> an exhaustive treatment of each topic [he wrote] is not intended; but simply the establishment of principles, with such illustrations as are needed to make their bearings fully understood.[10]

Please keep that in mind throughout this paper.

Having said all the things I shall *not* be doing it is now time I said more precisely what I *shall* do. I shall begin by stating an unconventional axiom—meaning by that something stronger than a proposition but less than a self-evident truth—and shall spend the rest of the lecture trying to prove it, beyond reasonable doubt. The proof will be approached in three ways, distinct but related, which will occupy respectively three sections of my talk. In the course of the demonstration it will, I hope, become clear why I think this approach appropriate to the memory of an evolutionist.

An unconventional axiom is commonly a neglected one, and it may well be wondered what axiom (if that *is* the right word) can possibly have been neglected in a topic so well covered as the medieval view of nature. It has, after all, been the subject of many studies, several of them classics, on subjects like, The Medieval Cosmos,[11] The Medieval Vision,[12] The Medieval Mind,[13] The Idea of Nature (in some medieval century),[14] The Discarded Image[15] (one of the classics), The Elizabethan World Picture[16] (another, and mostly medieval). With such coverage, you will ask, can any basic truth have been under-represented in respect of the medieval concept of nature? Yes, and this is it: *there wasn't one.*

This, then, is the axiom to be demonstrated beyond reasonable doubt. I shall do it by showing that there were several medieval concepts. Professor Lloyd argued a similar case for Greek thought.[17] But the demonstration here will take a different form. I shall rehearse three *kinds* of difference, each accounting for innumerable differences within its class. The three kinds will be called vertical, horizontal, and diagonal, each term to be explained in its place. Each will be shown to imply its own principle of resolution, the interaction of all of them providing the force, the *vis quaedam rebus insita*, which made medieval thought a process of continuous evolution. An analogy will help explain this purpose. Atomic physicists, not content to see the 'atom' any more as a unit, have analysed the distinct points of force within it, and by doing so explained the dynamic behaviour of the whole. I shall try to do the same.

THE VERTICAL DIVISION

We start, then, with the vertical division. This was the division which separated the views of people with different statuses. That word 'status' can be read several ways, for instance morally: habitually virtuous people, according to one persistent doctrine, thought differently about the world from the habitually vicious—the former, for instance, would attribute more to God, less to chance.[18] Again, it can be understood socially. That rich literary form of the late Middle Ages the sermon 'ad status'—directed towards this or that social class—can speak of similar divergences of belief as attaching to different social categories.[19] One vertical division, however, was more prominent than the rest, and is worth a moment's consideration. It was that between educated and uneducated.

Education after all, was partly *about* natural science. Relatively few people had it, even in the late Middle Ages, and they had had to acquire it. No one was born educated. So there must, necessarily, have been differences of view up and down the scale. A single example will show that there were. The earth looks flat, and many people, at least in the earlier Middle Ages, thought it was. A minstrel in *Beowulf*, for instance, related how

> God made the world a beautiful plain surrounded by sea.[20]

Beowulf has been variously dated between the early eighth century and the late eleventh. But it was certainly later than St. Isidore of Seville, who died in 636, knowing that the earth was spherical. Isidore's *Da natura rerum* and the *Etymologies* take this for granted. How Isidore knew it was from classical cosmologists, who had proved the earth's sphericity by the disappearance of ships over the horizon, the shadow on the moon at an eclipse, and by the different sets of stars seen as you move north or south.[21] Isidore's *De natura rerum* became the model for Bede's work of the same name, composed around 703, which went into at least 125 manuscripts, while the *Etymologies* were the medieval 'Larousse' and still survive in nearly a thousand copies.[22] So *Beowulf* and its circle had no excuse for ignorance; except that reading and writing were available to only a few, and that the shape of the earth was of at most qualified importance to the rest.

That is just one example of a division between learned and unlearned views. More could easily be found. A dramatic one is that of reactions to eclipses. A total eclipse of the sun could strike terror into some people, otherwise brave, if they had no idea that it represented regular natural movements. One such case occurred on 22 December 968, when German troops were besieging a Greek town in Calabria. The illiterate warriors, thinking the eclipse heralded the end of the world, hid themselves in terror until their bishop, who in youth had studied Pliny and other classical scientists, rallied them and urged them not to give such a cowardly impression to the Greeks since the eclipse, he told them, was a *res naturalis*.[23]

For our purposes this is not just a matter of educational 'haves' and 'have-nots'. The uneducated were also 'haves', in that they had their own positive views of nature. Most were peasants. If Montaillou is anything to go by—the Pyrenean village whose lives and thoughts were captured for posterity by Jacques Fournier's inquisition—peasants shared a front door with their pigs and cows.[24] They lived, in other words, in a proximity to nature unimaginable since the public health acts and Parker-Morris standards in housing—outside 'developing' countries, that is.

Such proximity to nature, together with a lack of book-learning, was bound to be reflected in the peasants' view of the natural world. A monk of Fleury-sur-Loire *c.*1050 described the peasants around there as 'semi-pagan'.[25] Originally that word *paganus* was the same word as 'peasant', and although the Fleury monk used it more specifically, meaning 'intellectually pre-Christian', he still reveals little of what the peasants actually believed. In this he is typical of medieval sources. Some of their reticence, however, has been breached by modern scholars, and their results can be summarized for present purposes under two headings.

The first is an astonishingly low level of abstraction. The Russian medievalist Aaron Gurevich found no abstract words of time or space in early Scandinavian languages. Thus an acre of land will be denoted by some word full of social implications, like 'an inheritance'. The notorious difficulties faced by early medieval scholars in tackling arithmetic may, perhaps, have been connected with such unfamiliarity, more-or-less inborn, with abstraction. So may Le Roy Ladurie's discovery, among the villagers of Montaillou, that they had no clear idea of anything outside their own immediate geographical area, or earlier than their great-grandfathers: they lived on what he called—on inspiration from Claude Lévi-Strauss—'une île de temps'.[26]

If a lack of abstraction was the first general feature of this 'mentalité primitive'—I choose that term as one already inoculated by the criticism evoked by Lévy-Bruhl's first use of it—the second was animism. Atlases with religious maps used to colour in large areas of the world as 'animist'; and the discredit which that clumsy anthropology drew on itself may lead us to think no one was ever 'animist': that is, believed soul and intelligence to obtain in parts of nature we think they do not. Yet there was certainly some, probably a lot, of such animism in medieval Europe. Around 1230, for instance, we hear a Paris philosopher, who had plenty else to spend his time on (and incidentally one whose origin in the Auvergne made him expert in popular beliefs), inveigh at length at people who think fire has a spirit in it and is alive.[27]

We have all heard of ordeal by fire, especially, in the medieval period, in the form of the hot iron, as of the comparable ordeal by water. It happens that a few years before that attack on fire-animism was written, senior churchmen had finally got together, in 1215, to withdraw church sanction for the judicial ordeal. Recent writing on the ordeal has not, to my knowledge, underlined the apparently animist character of its underlying beliefs. The official theory was that 'God' revealed the guilt or innocence of an accused 'through' the elements of fire and water. But comparison with hagiography and other sources suggests it was really the elements of fire and water which were acting on their own. They did not like impurity. The theory, in other words, was yet another Christian veneer.[28]

The same lesson can be learned from belief in spirits, described by the fully literate with the Greek word *daemones*. De Vries and other students of Germanic paganism have underlined the tendency in it to regard as holy, and as associated with spirits, certain immovable natural features like mountains or rivers; a tendency which (incidentally) made their conversion to Christianity easier when they were forced to migrate—for they could not take the features with them. Much of the topographic side of the medieval saint-cult bears interpretation as an attempt to erode such nature-bound religion; and even then, despite Winifred and her wells and Michael and his mountains, late-medieval synods still regularly denounce belief in the 'spirits' which haunt wells and springs.[29]

It may be cutting corners to dub all these beliefs simply 'animist'. But they suggest that spirit, with will and intelligence, is either in a physical object or closely attendant on it. An 'animist' reading to them, furthermore, would throw light on more puzzles in medieval belief than the few I have referred to, for instance, that well-known puzzle set by some uneducated reactions to Eucharistic theology, whereby in so-called eucharistic miracles the 'transubstantiated' species could be popularly *seen* as a living child.[30] If this reading is accepted then it only needs adding that education was meant to attenuate these beliefs. They were what you were educated from, and we learn of them for the most part from oblique or hostile references in written sources.

I hope to have shown, then, beyond reasonable doubt, that there were vertical divisions in medieval attitudes to nature. There were of course more than I have said. But the kind of division indicated, between those with and without education, will be enough to build the simple picture proposed here.

THE HORIZONTAL DIVISION

So we turn to a second type of division. This one is exclusively learned. It is found in the books that taught medieval scholars their natural philosophy, books whose authority they treated, to begin with at least, as much as a level whatever they were. So I have called this a 'horizontal' division.

The division will be again exemplified in two areas. The first is that of strictly classical tradition. For much of the Middle Ages learned views on the physical world were largely classical views. Long before the twelfth-century renaissance many of the basic doctrines—like the sphericity of the earth—had been available through late Latin résumés like that of Cassiodorus, and passed from these into dark-age encyclopaedias. When rising interest in the twelfth century brought a new wave of Latin translations these were mainly of classical works, enlarging the available canon. It is hard to overestimate the reverence of these earlier scholastic centuries for ancient science. We all know Bernard of Chartres' remark, made around 1120, that 'we are dwarfs, standing on giants' shoulders'. This remark is understood today as expressing humility. But many contemporaries heard it otherwise. Dwarfs had no business on giants' shoulders. Scientific knowledge was something that had been achieved in the past. *Moderni*—as they called themselves—could hardly hope to do more than recover it.

But then, within a decade or two of Bernard's remark, came a trauma. It shook academic Europe from Bologna to Paris, and after it things were never the same again. As more texts were studied by more people a dreadful truth began to dawn, slowly at first but soon with the clarity of day. *Ancient authorities did not always agree*. In Bologna the practical lawyers managed to contain the shock, as they learned how to reconcile their diverse authorities. In Paris, by contrast, the flamboyant Abelard in his *Yes and no* (*Sic et non*) flung a gauntlet at his contemporaries by setting out a series of blatant contradictions from patristic authorities, with nothing more attached than a set of theoretical instructions for their resolution. These instructions, nevertheless, contained in the prologue to *Sic et non*, formed a programme for the next century and a half, engendering what has been called the scholastic method. It was in fact many methods, but all had in common that they positively encouraged the expression of contrary opinions. The written deposit of Paris philosophy in this period bristles with devices for articulating opinions other than the author's—even if, like so many chickens in a coop, they were sometimes preserved only to have their necks wrung summarily when the author gave his own answer.

The system for conserving multiple opinions was not originally designed for natural science. But as Greek and Arabic science flooded into Latin, roughly between 1140 and 1240, its own fissures came with it and lodged themselves in the scholastic apparatus. To explore even a few of them would be to enter a library. Miss Annaliese Maier alone filled eight or nine volumes with her studies of single *quaestiones* on natural problems.[31]

Without entering any libraries a single example, once more, will be enough to show that kind of division is in question.[32] A basic problem of all pre-modern science was how the stars stay up; how, that is, they stay up without our seeing what holds them up, and in such a way as to permit their movement. The problem of movement was most acute in the cause of the 'wanderers' or 'tramps' (Greek πλανετες). Aristotle had taught that heavenly bodies were on huge balls, or spheres made of some invisible substance like heavenly glass, which resolved concentrically with no space between, so that they supported each other. That fitted with the rest of Aristotelian physics; but only imperfectly, as it proved, with observation. The problem was the wandering planets. In the next four-and-a-half centuries Greek mathematicians had made closer observations and came up with a theory which fitted better with what they saw. The planets, said the theory, moved in epicycles round a main orbit or deferent. The only trouble with the theory at that stage was its inconsistency with Aristotle. For if the planets moved on epicycles, their planes along an earthly observer's line of sight, they would smash any glass balls they were meant to be nesting in. The epicyclic theory is associated with Ptolemy of Alexandria, who died around AD 170, though he may have relied heavily on his predecessor Hipparchus.

At all events, the disagreement was still there when the question was inherited by medieval philosophy. Ptolemy's theory became known between 1137 and 1175, at first indirectly and later in good translations of his *Almagest*—testimonies to the appeal his theory had for astronomers. But around the latter of these dates translators were also working on Aristotle's *libri naturales*, as the scientific works were called. These swept into Paris in a flood lasting from around then until the 1230s, covering all subjects imaginable: zoology, botany, geology, meteorology, and (of course) astronomy. Contradiction was now standing on the bookshelf. Some people did not notice it, and upheld both theories as true, which they could not be. Those who took sides veered to Aristotle. For how could so omniscient a naturalist have been wrong? They did not see that Ptolemy represented over four centuries' more progress in Greek mathematics. Thus medieval science itself went into retrograde motion, like a planet, for much of the thirteenth century. Finally, observation recovered the initiative, partly because of popular taste for astrological prediction, and restored Ptolemy's credit. Refining it and refining it, with new epicycles and adjustments to fit their ever more patient observations (some of which had to extend as much as two years)[33] they elaborated Ptolemaic theory for two more centuries until, under a single smart blow from Copernicus, the whole, increasingly complicated system would be turned inside out to produce the elegant heliocentric theory we accept now.

This 'horizontal' division between Aristotelian and Ptolemaic planetary theory has served a purpose. It has shown the *kind* of division which medieval learning inherited from ancient, as Greek science was recovered; and it has shown how, within a system designed to debate doubtful questions, and despite the inertias usual in the history of science, the doubt was eventually worked out.

But I said I would examine these horizontal divisions in two areas. Classical philosophy was only the first; and I have described it as if it were a dead, static wreck, raised complete with its fissures from a dark-age sea bed. Philosophies cannot in fact last like that. Like the brains that think them they must always have oxygen, the breath of life, not least—though not only—because texts need recopying (especially any on papyrus). Ancient philosophy had in fact been alive throughout the western European Dark Ages, but elsewhere than in Europe. And if alive, then also growing: at the time of its encounter with scholasticism classical natural philosophy had grown conspicuously, in fact, at its two conceptual extremities, religious and mathematical. This double-ended growth is the second feature we have to consider in the philosophy that medieval thinkers inherited.

It fell in two phases, roughly before and after the seventh century, phases which reflect the whole sweep of Mediterranean history after Augustus. The first starts in Alexandria when, denied political supremacy. Alexandria became an academic powerhouse and Platonic tradition fused there with local religious currents to enhance the religious element in Platonism. The world of sense was relegated to the status of, at best, a stepping stone to a graded series of invisible worlds, culminating in the One, from whom all causation emanated. The father of this interpretation was Plotinus, who lived in the third century. He thought himself a Platonist. Historians have called him a Neoplatonist. The philosophy of his school may have represented a deliberate riposte by ancient philosophy to the challenge of the *enfant terrible*, Christianity. The riposte failed. But, as often, the loser affected the winner. Not only did some of the transmitters of ancient thought, like Macrobius and Chalcidius (who translated Plato) tinge it with Neoplatonism; but also two thinkers so obscure that no one knew who they were ended by acting as Neoplatonist 'moles' in the heart of medieval thought. One was the author of *De causis* a work later prominent on Dante's shelf, among others'. It was believed, by another massive anachronism, to be by Aristotle, but was in fact an abbreviation of a dense, late summary of Neoplatonist doctrine by the fifth-century Athenian Proclus. The other was the author now called 'Pseudo-Denys' or 'Pseudo-Dionysius', probably a Syrian of the early sixth century whose writings, a group of mystical treatises, got from him or someone shortly after him an attribution to St. Paul's convert Dionysius the Areopagite, mentioned in Acts. He, too, was closely dependent on Proclus.[34]

I shall return to Pseudo-Denys. But it is time to follow the development of ancient philosophy into its second phase, after the seventh century. Between 636 and 711 Muslim Arabs conquered the lands between Spain and Sind. Paradoxically, perhaps, in a religion sometimes conspicuous for doctrinal rigorism, the structure of Muslim authority was such as to allow, as the conquests became a distant memory, considerable philosophical freedom. From former Persian and Greek soil Islam inherited rich intellectual currents. Babylonian astrology was still alive at Harran on the Euphrates, and with the help of the numerals we now call Arabic, imported from just over the frontier in India, the mathematical side of Greek philosophy was developed further. In Syria, already in Syriac when the Arabs conquered it, had been Aristotle. Most important of all, in a culture expressly religious, was Plato, in largely Neoplatonist garb. What specialists have called an 'aristotélisme néoplatonisant' was especially strong in the Persian philosopher Ibn Sina, who died in 1037, and would later be known in Latin as Avicenna.[35]

It is tempting to call this Arabic philosophy Islamic, and this is right in the sense that the philosophers were Muslims, more or less devout. (The celebrated Averroes was thought so *un*devout that he was hounded into exile before his death in 1198.) But there is a danger. The points in Arabic philosophy which grated with Christianity, when the time came, usually grated also with Islam, and for that matter Judaism. At least they should have done. For what was at stake was the relation of the world with God, and doctrines on this have a strong family resemblance in the three traditions. Let it be enough to call this second phase of development Arabic, after the language it was written in, and to recognize it and its mathematics as a second addition, with late Greek Neoplatonism, to the living tradition of ancient philosophy. Both additions, of course, had *their* 'horizontal' fissures, too, debated by their devotees. But I have sought, like Spencer, only to 'establish principles', not exhaust their illustration; and it is time to turn to a third kind of division in medieval thought.

I have described these post-classical developments in ancient philosophy as extending its two conceptual extremities. Neoplatonism, that is to say, sought to define more closely the unseen, spiritual world; while mathematical astronomers gave the world of sense-phenomena the most systematic inspection it had yet had. At the moment of its encounter with western Christendom, therefore, in the twelfth and thirteenth centuries, the philosophical tradition was at its maximum extent. It covered everything: man, the world, the stars; and what might be beyond man, beyond even the world and the stars. The Christian religion had begun with simple fishermen. It was now in the hands of Germanic Europeans still half sunk in their mentalité primitive. In the late twelfth and early thirteenth centuries it had to confront this philosophy; to convert it or be converted. The encounter was like that which modern geology ascribes to the tectonic plates that form the earth's surface, whose concourse moulds the continents on which we live. It will be the subject of the third and last section of this lecture.

THE DIAGONAL DIVISION

I hope to have demonstrated, beyond reasonable doubt, the existence of two sorts of division among medieval views of nature: between those of the mass of people and those of persons in some way educated; and among the latter, between the very strands of their education. I now turn to a third kind of division: that between what was consistent, and what was not consistent, with Christianity. The distinctions in this class moved and resolved themselves around a core of central doctrines, a core which touched both the learned and the unlearned and bound their concerns together. Because a diagonal, placed between two planes at 45°, belongs to both of them, I have called this set of differences 'diagonal'; but not in order to pick a quarrel about a term.

Not that term, at least. But I have spoken of 'Christianity', and will start by defining it more closely as an historical factor in the present connection. This is best done by speaking of the medieval context in which its traditions survived, and of its general nature as a religion.

Christianity: its context and nature

I suggested earlier that it was hard for us in the late twentieth century to imagine the hugger-mugger of those pigs and peasants. It is equally hard to imagine the circumstances, often comfortably away from pigs and peasants, in which most medieval intellectuals did their thinking, about nature or anything else. Efforts of imagination in this regard will be made easier, however, by two brief reflections.

One concerns the liturgy. Although that word is basically modern the fact is so medieval that it was called the 'office', which meant simply 'the job'. By the time of the twelfth century renaissance, it is true, monks—the liturgical specialists—were losing their learned hegemony to urban schools. But most masters in towns still had liturgical obligations. St. Victor, for instance, powerhouse of the Paris renaissance, was an Augustinian priory; Peter Chanter, doyen of Paris masters at the end of the century, *was* a chanter, in Notre Dame. The same was doubly true when the friars took up residence in the universities in the 1220s. Their rules might limit liturgical duties to accommodate learning, but that only shows what a lot remained.[36]

There were many reasons why liturgy should shape its devotees' thought about nature. The most palpable was timing—synchronization being the essence of liturgical worship. Before there were proper clocks (a fourteenth-century invention) someone had to observe the heavens carefully to get the liturgy synchronized.[37] But even if you were not the timekeeper the sequence of the 'hours', each with references in hymns and prayers to the appropriate changes of the day, meant the liturgy kept you thinking about the physical world—noon, sunset, and so on. Candles, furthermore, were an expense; and this, besides the relatively greater role it left for the sky, meant that much of the liturgy would come to be known by heart, and that augmented the force with which repetition stamped the meaning of the liturgy on the minds involved. This message, I repeat, was partly about nature. But it was not about nature on its own; but about nature *in relation to* its creator and sustainer, God. Here, as just one of innumerable examples, is a snatch to show the sort of thing:

> Fire, and hail; snow, and vapours; stormy wind fulfilling his word: Mountains, and all hills, beasts, and all cattle. . . . Praise . . . the Lord (Ps. 147/8.8–12).

That is from Lauds, sung as dawn approached. Now it also happens to be from the Bible, as most liturgical texts were. And the second of my two brief reflections is that most serious medieval intellectuals knew the Bible well. The reflection is the more worth making because its substance has in the past sometimes been denied, so that some people thought it was Wyclif who discovered the Bible, until the late Beryl Smalley put everyone straight. Liturgy apart, the Bible was expounded in sermons, to which Paris scholars were supposed to listen regularly. As for the post-graduates who took theology, they had to know the *divina pagina* thoroughly, often (again) hearing lectures in bad light so that they had to memorize texts. This biblical knowledge too had consequences for its possessors' outlook on nature. One was the same as in the case of liturgy: the Bible said plenty about nature, but always in terms of a relationship between it and God. There was also a more specifically intellectual consequence. I have said enough of horizontal divisions, but plenty more could (if I had not) be found in the text of the Bible, which is a palimpsest of ancient cosmologies, each with its differences. It has to be. For religious tradition is by definition enduring; God speaks to successive generations in an idiom appropriate to each; and idioms change. The Bible therefore set physical puzzles for commentators long before they read Greek science. What, for instance, were those 'waters above the heavens' of Psalm 148 (when everyone knows water flows downhill)? Or 'the ends of the round world' of Psalm 18? And why did Genesis give two different accounts (in 1:27 and 2:17 and 22) of the creation of Adam and Eve? And so on.

These questions were the stuff of the 'horizontal' divisions debated by biblical students before the scientific renaissance began in earnest, and remained so. They formed the adit to the broader-based *quaestiones naturales* which summoned Greek and Arabic science to their aid. This explains much about medieval physical views: they never lost traces of this origin.

Something like a third of continuous cosmological speculation in the period is contained in commentaries of Genesis (known as the 'hexameral tradition'). The *questiones* studied so voluminously by Miss Maier were largely based on commentaries on Peter Lombard's *Sentences*, a strictly theological work (written around 1150); and numerous scientific concepts, later the stock-in-trade of seventeenth-century physics, began and long endured in theological contexts. An example is impetus, the idea of a *vis impressa*, 'force imprinted', on a body by a 'mover', which remains in the body when the mover has gone. The physical concept of *vis impressa* was born in the context of discussions of the imparting of a soul to the human seed or fetus, and of the quality added to the Eucharist at consecration.[38]

In terms of its human context, then, the encounter between Latin Christianity and Greek-Arabic natural philosophy took place in minds fed by meditative reflection on liturgical and biblical texts. I have described this intellectual milieu as 'Christianity', and have done so to avoid a cliché. It is often said that it was 'the church' that rejected unorthodox doctrines—as if there was a group of men with reversed collars enduring throughout history when all else changed, who told people what they could and could not think. The hierarchy, if that is what is meant, was usually much too inefficient for that. In any broader sense all the Christian philosophers in question, orthodox and unorthodox, were in 'the church'. The process by which doctrines were taken or rejected by Christian tradition was in fact, as I have tried to indicate, a subtler, more communal affair, and one attendant on impulses less from bishops, as such, than from the deepest levels of prayerful thought.

This understood, we can now pose our question. What, in its encounter with Greek-Arabic ideas of nature, did scholastic Christianity digest, and what reject, and why? How did it establish, in other words, across those other two planes of division, its own, diagonal, distinction, of ideas to be raised into, or cast out of, accepted philosophical canon?

My answer will be confined to the encounter of Christianity with the two main foci of Greek thought, Plato and Aristotle, the thinkers whose fundamental similarities, and fundamental differences, are the most constant single theme in western intellectual history. But the impact of those two Greek thinkers on Christianity will only be understood if a certain strong peculiarity of this religion is understood first.

Like its founder, Christianity has two natures, apparently in contradiction but both necessary. To the *homme moyen sensuel* its more obvious nature is the one that keeps telling him to be less greedy, to think more of God and the next life. To the historian of religion, however, that is not unique to Christianity: most of its early rivals, and most Christian heresies, would say the same. Christianity has not only an otherworldly nature, but a *this*-worldly nature too. God made the world, saw it was good, and when man had ruined it God came into the world, healed people and told them how to live in the world and then, by dying as he did, reconciled the world to God again, giving the whole cosmos unity. (This very last point was made by Robert Grosseteste, and Sir Richard Southern has elegantly shown how it bound his theology with his natural science.[39])

The double nature in Christianity has governed its approach to views originating elsewhere. Each nature has an appetite, bidding it digest what is appropriate; and each has a 'veto', stopping its partner, in obeying that appetite, from digesting what might injure itself. The explanation of this simple formula may be less simple than the formula and therefore I shall summarize my explanation before giving it.

It was Christianity's *otherworldly* self that digested Plato and his tradition; and its *this*-worldly self that digested Aristotle. Conversely, when Platonic conclusions endangered the this-worldly character of Christianity, it rejected them; and vice-versa for Aristotle. This principle, I shall argue, underlies the development of scholastic views on the natural world. It also, as it should, explains in passing the semantic history of the word 'nature'. For it was this double encounter that engendered its two meanings; one, with a capital 'N', drew its force from Platonic tradition and did so with no opposition from Christianity because tempered by another, with a small 'n', which was nourished by Aristotle. Finally—since nature stands in antithesis to will and intelligence, and these last are the subject of 'animism'—I shall say how both Aristotle and Plato, in quite different ways, sublimated the animism of the mentalité primitive; but neither quite enough for Christianity. There the dwarf *did* stand on the giant's shoulders; and saw further.

Plato and the other world

That is the summary. In dressing it out in more detail I begin with Christianity as an otherworldly religion, and with Platonist tradition. This tradition made one undisputed contribution, one ambivalent contribution, and one serious mistake—from a Christian angle.

The undisputed contribution was an encouragement to study the world and its workings, because divine secrets were to be read there. The idea was native to Christianity. Jesus had referred to weather-forecasting by the look of the sky and said people should see by themselves what was right, without his teaching (Mt.16:2–4). St. Paul wrote that the 'invisible things of God' could be learned from created things (in a passage, Rom.1:20, which would often appear in medieval scientific contexts as a reason—or a pretext?—for studying it).[40] The Fathers took this up, each in the way suggested by his school or cast of mind. The Alexandrians, not surprisingly, gave it their own emphasis. So did St. Augustine, whose *De doctrina christiana* wove it into his influential apologia for the study of nature within a religious culture.[41] The idea would pass into scholasticism. Two of its strongest representatives would be Hugh of St. Victor, whose *Didascalicon* (*Education*) would be a blueprint for higher education, and whose famous motto was 'learn everything'; and in the next century Thomas Aquinas, who taught that careful study of phenomena could take you to the threshold of revelation—though not over it, as would be held by the more diehard advocates of 'natural religion' in the eighteenth century.

Although native to Christianity this idea was enriched by Neoplatonist influence, through several channels. It is best seen through the posthumous career of that sixth-century Syrian I mentioned earlier, Pseudo-Denys. The career has both an inner and an outer aspect, each of which fed the other: that is, Denys' writings, and the legend of his life.

From its translation into Latin in the ninth century, by the Irish-born Erigena, Pseudo-Denys' *The celestial hierarchy* offered an intense version of the theme in question. Our word 'analogy' enters western language through Erigena's ninth-century translation, or rather non-translation, of this Greek Neoplatonist word. Its dense background can best be judged by an example. In one place Pseudo-Denys compares fire and divine love. The nature (*natura*) of fire, he says, is inherently *like* that of love.

> Fire can blaze up suddenly and die down as suddenly. It can be almost invisible yet keep its infinite potential, to burn all it touches, leaping up anything combustible brought near it. Fire grows by exercise; casts dazzling light on things in shadow; bears upwards what it touches . . .

So it goes on. Some of the original passage, which I have heavily summarized, comes within a hair's breadth of poetry.[42]

That was the inner aspect of Denys' career. (In medieval style let us now drop the 'Pseudo'.) The inner aspect developed in symbiosis with an outer: Denys' legend as told in *The golden legend* and other late-medieval collections. This legend involved one of the most pregnant confusions in the history of European thought, a confusion which, like most past mistakes, serves for historical instruction. Its first element you have heard: the confusion between the sixth-century admirer of Proclus and St. Paul's disciple Dionysius the Areopagite. This compound figure was then merged with that of a third Denys, an evangelist of Paris in the third century, in whose honour the abbey of St. Denys had been raised. The story in Acts was then expanded. Being Greek, it now ran, Dionysius had of course been an astronomer. As such he must have observed the eclipse at Christ's death and recognized it as not a natural eclipse. So he concluded that the God of nature must have died, and erected an altar to this 'unknown God' (that altar, by the way, *is* in Acts). Paul merely told him who this God was. Finally, St. Denys had brought Christianity to Paris, the new, Christian 'Athens'. More even than the story of the Magi (who found Christ by observing the sky), the legend of St. Denys, like his writings, served as a permanent encouragement to medieval scholars to study natural science. It is no accident that both the two philosophers I have just mentioned, Hugh of St. Victor and Thomas Aquinas, are prominent on the list of medieval commentators on Denys.[43]

Denys represents the undisputed contribution of Platonist tradition to medieval philosophy. The next contribution was ambivalent. It concerns Creation. Plato had seen the world of nature as all movement. It could not contain the timeless, unmoving principle which gave it origin. So it must have been created. Plato's account of creation in the *Timaeus* had an uncanny resemblance to that in Genesis, enough for scholars to think Plato had actually got it from Moses, by some obscure channel across the eastern Mediterranean. It is only a bare exaggeration to say that medieval speculation on the character of the cosmos began when scholars associated with Chartres, in and just after the time of that Bernard of Chartres, made diligent comparisons between the two texts. But Plato's doctrine of creation proved in the end to have limitations. It gave little help in the knotty question of whether *matter* had been created, or only put in order. And when it came to be most needed, in the thirteenth century, the Platonic idea of creation came apart in the church's hands; because by then a Neoplatonist interpretation had gained ascendency which made creation timeless, a continuous emanation with no 'big bang' to start with: not good enough, as we shall see.[44]

There was a second problem with the idea of creation in the *Timaeus*. Like our semi-pagan peasants Plato did not think man was the only repository in the natural world of will and intelligence. Plato thought the world itself had these. The cosmos had a soul. If it did not have eyes and ears that was because there was nothing to see or hear outside itself: and nothing for hands to hold, feet on or stomach to digest. But it was alive, for all that. Again, this notion of an omnipresent vital force had such a striking resemblance to one aspect of the Christian idea of God that some scholars, at the beginning, thought Plato must have discovered the Holy Spirit—no doubt by a similar route to that of his other discoveries, that is, from the Jewish prophets. Plato had certainly sublimated the animism of those medieval 'semi-pagans'. But the sublimation did not go quite far enough. Critics pointed out that Plato's *Anima mundi* was itself created, so could not be the Holy Spirit. So the idea had to be dropped, or rather, harmlessly redeployed. For parallels in language, and the close dependence of a small group of contemporary texts suggest that it was Plato's *Anima mundi*, thus disappointed of divine status, which fathered that allegorical figure of Natura.[45]

The idea of the world as a 'sign', then, was accepted. Plato's doctrine of creation was accepted in parts. Finally, Platonist tradition fell thoroughly foul of Christianity in one major respect. When a bishop of Paris condemned 219 heterodox 'opinions' in 1277, 'opinion' number three read:

> That God knows of nothing but himself.[46]

This reflected a contemporary school of thought traceable to Avicenna, and his 'aristotélisme néo-platonisant'. The idea was that God was the pure source of a long river, separated from its turbulent estuary by a series of graded waterfalls, and therefore unaware of it. Readers of Arthur Lovejoy's *The great chain of being* will recognize this notion.[47] In Neoplatonism the higher grades of causation can only reach the lower through an intermediary. In this form the doctrine put a distance between God and this world, and thus offended against Jewish, Muslim, *and* Christian views. Their God had two natures, sublime *and* interested in minutiae. They knew there was a contradiction here, and that their revelation was an exception. As Psalm 112 says:

> Who is like the Lord our God, who has his dwelling so high and yet looks at the humble things of heaven and earth?

It is not our business here to ask how the contrary doctrine survived in a Muslim milieu; only to note that it was repelled by thirteenth-century Christian thought for making a nonsense, among other things, of the Gospel.[48]

One thing it made a nonsense of in the Gospel was the miracles. I shall say more about miracles. But before that we must turn from Plato, and his emphasis on the Other World, to look more generally at the *this*-worldly aspect of Christianity, and its striking medieval partnership with Aristotle.

Aristotle and *this* world

In European thought Aristotle has had fewer quarrels than Plato with religion, and more with science, which shows that like quarrels with like. Since Aristotle had known nothing of Christianity and did not even have what antiquity would have seen as strong religious instincts, he was accommodated in Christian thought with an ease that may seem surprising, and must have done to those who watched the scared prelates who, right at the beginning of the thirteenth century, had met the intellectual giant at the door and tried to bar it against him.[49] In due course not only was Aristotle let in, but his thought was partially 'baptized', so much so that in the early modern period opposition to Aristotle could invite a charge of impiety (of all things).

In a moment I shall consider reasons for this partial 'baptism' of a pagan philosopher. However, reversing the order of my treatment of Plato, it will be best to look first at what Christianity saw as the greatest of Aristotle's errors— the part that was not baptized. The error concerned creation. Aristotle's difference from Plato on this matter derived less from the data they worked from than from temperament. Unlike his teacher Plato, who depreciated this world's ever-changing phenomena, Aristotle was fascinated by them. He found their changes so regular that he saw no reason why they should ever come to an end or, for the same reason. should ever have begun. Since there were astronomical reasons—partly from the earlier civilization of Babylon—for thinking the world had gone on and would go on for ever, that was the position Aristotle took.[50] There *was* no Creation. Those medieval scholars who viewed Aristotle with such bedazzled reverence that they thought him right on all natural questions agreed even on this. Averroes was principal among them. But not only was this quite unacceptable to anyone who believed in the Semitic God. Even the historian is bound to wonder whether history after the thirteenth century would not have been different if Aristotle's view had—by some unimaginable turn of events—prevailed. For the doctrine of creation gave time what is called a 'vectoral' character: it was going somewhere, rather than in circles. Those familiar with the thought and technology of the period, with its interest in history and in prophecies, its calendars and clocks, would I hope agree that the matter of vectoral time was no small one.

That was where Aristotle fell short of medieval Christianity and it rejected him. In most other respects he was an ally; and in one in particular. To see its importance we must look more closely at one of the most significant, and one still mysterious, feature of medieval religious thought: miracles.

A heterodox opinion condemned by the bishop of Paris in 1277, it was said a moment ago, was that God knows of nothing down here in the world. This doctrine met more formidable resistance than that of any bishop. It ran up against miracles, or rather a widespread belief and attention to them. As well as in the Bible these miracles mostly appear in saints' Lives and related literature. There are 28 thousand extant saints' Lives and most have many miracles each.[51] So there were a lot. The great majority were cures. What they showed was that God did care for the world, even so-and-so's sore foot. The Lives, it is true, often related the miracles as if the saint had done it, and it is fair, within limits, to see these Lives as a Christian response to non-Christian ideas of magic and magicians.[52] The doctrine nevertheless remained inviolate, in and out of the Lives, that it was ultimately God who did the miracles, through and for the saint. They were therefore a constant reminder of God's knowledge of the world and concern even for its minutiae. On a non-academic level the radically dualist Cathars, the extreme wing of the Albigensian heresy, rejected miracles for just this reason: the world was too bad for the good God to intervene in it.[53]

Now miracles presented an intellectual problem. Of course they are meant to. Part of the idea of miracles, for theologians, is that they challenge assumptions. There has never been a time—certainly not in the Middle Ages (to go by protests in miracle-literature against the incredulous)—when everyone believed all the miracles. So there were always assumptions to be challenged. But the intellectual problem I refer to is not that. It is one more of definition. The word miracle is derived from *miror*, 'I wonder at'. That makes a miracle just something amazing. For many centuries the term *miracula* was used for things like Seven Wonders of the World, known by dark-age scholars as the *miracula mundi*.

St. Augustine of Hippo had enshrined this subjective notion of miracle in his definitions. In the work quoted at the beginning of this lecture, for instance, *The use of believing*, he says a miracle is *quidquid arduum est aut insolitum supra spem vel facultatem mirantis apparet*: 'whatever is hard or appears unusual beyond the expectation or comprehension of the observer.'[54] The Augustinian definition long served as the basis for most others. But in the twelfth and thirteenth centuries subtle changes occurred, changes chronicled by the leading historian of the subject, Alois Van Hove. As if by a slip of the pen the term 'nature' kept creeping into definitions, in the context of phrases like 'against the common course of nature'. The change occurs in several writers, each with his own phraseology, while in Aquinas the term 'supernatural' first enters the European vocabulary in this sense. For them, the *arduum* and *insolitum* of Augustine's definition of miracle were to be read as meaning that it was *contra consuetum cursum naturae*.[55]

Now here *is* the intellectual problem. For the definition of miracle as an exception to laws of nature begs a big question, namely what a law of nature is. If it is an observed regularity, and no more, then any exception merely proves the regularity has not been properly observed and a new law must be formulated to include the exception. To pretend that a law of nature is more than that, on the other hand, is to make a statement about nature, one hard if not impossible to prove. The name of T. H. Huxley, Herbert Spencer's contemporary, is associated with this objection. But it was one inherent in the scholastic idea of miracle from the start. As early as the generation after Aquinas, philosophical sceptics had raised comparable doubts, challenging the certainty of all human knowledge about nature, and hence, implicitly, the idea that miracle could be an exception to known natural laws.[56]

But the history of ideas, like that of politics, involves a balance of forces; and for all its precarious elements the scholastic idea of miracle remained strong in the late Middle Ages, with important consequences. I shall end this paper by suggesting a reason why. It is that miracle, thus defined, harmonized with a certain way of apprehending nature, a way shared, despite all I have said on divisions—vertical, horizontal or diagonal—in medieval views on nature, by most of those who held them, forming the conceptual language of their disagreements.

In leaving this task till the end of my lecture I am conscious of 'rushing things'. In so far as my thesis rises above the banal it may appear ill-defined, or simply wrong. But I hope an attempt to summarize it may at least give us something to think about. It is that medieval people generally saw nature as essentially multiple: an aggregate, that is to say, of individual 'things', each with its properties, each with its own 'nature'. *Prima facie* witnesses are some of those titles of medieval books about nature. Hexameral commentaries apart, the commonest single form of title is that of *De naturis rerum*; *De proprietatibus rerum*. Even the singular *De natura rerum* leaves the *rerum*, the plural 'things', whose individual 'properties' are in question.[57] Not only are singular titles like *De universo* or *Megacosmos* rarer. Their authors generally reveal, inside the book, that they knew their title has a point to make.[58]

But the plural outlook on nature I am suggesting went deeper than book-titles. It drew on many sources, few of them peculiar to the Middle Ages, but coming together then with an effect peculiar to the period. For the educated, a basic source was the book of Genesis itself. Some of the others will be visible through commentary on it. 'In the beginning' God had made the species, the 'things'. Genesis implied that whatever number of species God had made, remained their number, and that implication was duly drawn, so that it was even debated whether God *could* have made more or fewer than he did. It was as if the number of 'things' was not merely experienced empirically, but was fixed in eternity before Creation,[59] and also after Creation. For those 'things' which were alive, and hence (unlike rocks or sea) might fade away and disappear, were programmed by the Creator to reproduce, each according to its kind. This biblical doctrine struck a resonance with a Stoic one, that of the *ratio seminalis*, the 'principle of the seed', which accounted for the emergence of the oak tree from the acorn and could be extended far beyond botany.[60] By explaining change, the doctrine of *ratio seminalis* served to reconcile the concept of fixed species with the baffling mutability of actual appearances, even in inanimate objects.

Not least among lessons of Genesis was that when the species were made Adam had given them names (Gen 2:19–20). In the Middle Ages this text struck root in what may be called a 'dictionary' view of knowledge. The 'Larousse' status of Isidore's *Etymologies* is one testimony to this. Another is a more general fascination with etymologies (as in *The golden legend*, which begins each legend with one). According to this 'dictionary view', not only is there a word for everything but every word has a thing corresponding to it. Much in the evolution of medieval philosophy can be seen as the growing-pains of this idea, most conspicuously in Nominalism. Nominalists insisted that the existence of *nomina*, names, does not imply an equal measure of reality in what they refer to. The lesson for historians is that this needed to be said.[61]

A lot more could be said about this 'plurality' among the educated. But it probably began before education. Rustic 'animism' itself may have played the first part. For while neglecting one boundary—between animate and inanimate—the attribution of spirit to things reinforced many more boundaries, namely between the spirits, of (say) this or that river, tree, and so on, so that these 'things' took on some of the irreducible plurality of human individuals; and this much, at least, of the intellectual consequences of rustic animism could survive even the strictest education. Robbed of most of its spirits, nature could still keep much of their essential plurality.

Even partial acceptance of this thesis would place us better to appreciate the appeal of Aristotle. It would make him, for the intellectual milieu in question, the perfect schoolmaster. *Par excellence* an empirical observer, Aristotle knew that we do, in fact, first apprehend the world as a variety of distinct 'things', whose properties have to be learned one by one. (I mean 'we', still: as small children, and long before we read Stephen Hawking.) Aristotle was thus able to provide for medieval students an intellectual 'software' appropriate to their existing mentality. At its base was 'hylemorphism', a distinction of matter and form (*hyle*, *morphe*), such that when you see a table the form enters your mind but not the matter (the timber would damage your eye). By 'dividing' and 'composing' these forms the intellect attained knowledge of the 'substantial forms'—tables as such, furniture as such. It did not matter if nominalists said the substantial 'table' was unreal. The system gave all philosophers an ordered device for making abstractions from nature. For two centuries in all disciplines, and in some (notably biology) much longer, the device for abstraction remained fundamental to the physical discussion, better able to take root because its plurality—its substantial forms were a multitude, like the species of Genesis and like them fixed in number—reflected on a philosophical level the pattern of thought already present to his medieval readers, certainly from their schooldays, possibly from their infancy. Most of them, after all, whether or not they had slept next to the cows, were a kind of amateur biologist—like Aristotle.[62]

Now this 'multiple' view of nature was unstable. Aristotle had sought and found more general principles to link 'things' together: like the doctrine of four 'elements', and rules of change which were themselves constant. Medieval Aristotelians strenuously took this search further.[63] Outside the schools, meanwhile, the same search for connections between 'things' was pursued in the world of practical experiment by alchemists' attempts to change one thing into another; and in that of poetry by (for instance) the appeal—greater than before or since—of Ovid's *Metamorphoses*, whose episodes dwell, with a fascination appropriate to a challenged taboo, on imagined changes between species, animate and inanimate.

The restiveness duly produced results, and in the areas where it did so new ways of looking at nature would be born, destined to surpass Aristotle. In modern science the most conspicuous breaches of the 'multiple' view of nature would be those by Darwin and by the physical chemists. But the erosion had already begin in the Middle Ages. Aristotle's treatment of the sublunary and superlunary parts of the cosmos as two things, with different properties, was already challenged by Grosseteste's theory of light, which behaved the same in both spheres. But the most conspicuous agent of erosion would be mathematics, which gradually detached and—as it were—privatized to itself those areas of natural philosophy appropriate for its rigorous treatment. Its first field of action was astronomy, *alias* astrology. As long as it kept clear of its endemic temptation to determinism astrology was allowed to develop those skills with 'Arabic' arithmetic which were there ready to serve the next layers when the time came: dynamics, then mechanics generally, in a 'mechanization of the world-picture' now well-chronicled by E. J. Dijksterhuis. But here too the change was not just academic. The advance of mathematics, like the plural view of nature itself, obtained far outside the schools; for instance, in a general tendency to reduce names to numbers, as in dating, and—apparently more slowly—in such fields as points of the compass (which the early Middle Ages knew as twelve individual 'winds', each with its name and character).[64]

While it lasted, the 'multiple' nature of the Middle Ages served a function so important that it is hard to conceive later European intellectual development without it. For natural science to grow within a Christian matrix an accommodation was needed between the idea of physical laws, and that of God's direct interest and power in nature. The 'multiple' view of nature offered this accommodation. For it not only allowed, but positively encouraged, the idea that physical laws, regular enough to admit investigation, kept enough palpable irregularity to accommodate a belief in mysterious powers.

This double quality can be neatly demonstrated in the medieval treatment of two questions, back-to-back elaborations of the same issue. One is natural necessity. As the idea of physical laws became more deeply lodged during the thirteenth century the question arose whether physical laws *have* to work as they do?[65] If the answer was 'yes', it was agreed, then the God-excluding determinism that astronomers were being told to avoid would invade physics more generally. But the answer was 'no'; and what saved the day was the 'multiple' approach to nature. For it made easy the proof that nature*s*, in the plural, did *not* work by necessity. For instance, it is in the nature of fire to rise, and it usually does. But not if you block the chimney. So its nature cannot work by necessity, QED. This proof was employed by no less exalted a philosopher than Aquinas.[66] It would have needed a more comprehensive, non-plural, approach to natural laws to pose the further question whether, it being in the nature of blockages to block, they block by necessity.

The same multiple approach solved the same problem in reverse: namely, whether divine interventions in natural laws can actually happen. Thinkers who tackled this problem could reply that exceptions to natural law were *always* happening. For instance, the nature of a stone is to crack in heat. But asbestos does not. It is the nature of water to fall. But water will rise up the sides of a pipette. *Divide et impera.*[67] When natures were thus divided it was easy to see their power as contingent. Just as pluralism in medieval society allowed ecclesiastical privilege, so natural pluralism lodged a concept of causation that allowed both an intervening God *and* natural laws; and hence both science *and* a religious culture.

It is time to conclude. We have watched medieval Christianity choosing judiciously between Aristotle and Plato. The final ascendency of mathematics looks at first like a new victory for Plato, prophet of the truth latent behind appearances. But for a true

Platonist mathematics is not latent enough: however beautiful its truth it is still intelligible, man-size. The development of science since the Middle Ages has, in fact, disengaged it from both its great Greek pilots—from the stern religious intuition of the one and the common-sense this-worldiness of the other.

The disengagement has posed problems, still with us, perhaps more than we realize. It has not been my task to contribute directly to their solution, only to sketch, in outline, the geometry of the views of nature from which they emerged—a geometry with its vertical, horizontal, and diagonal divisions, and the Spencerian evolution generated by the tensions between them. The following papers will show that our modern views of nature are ultimately continuous with those of our ancestors, including those I have discussed here. So I hope this geometry lesson has taught some useful indirect lessons.

One of its lessons, however, remains. We have learned that medieval people had plenty to disagree about; disagreement is a kind of doubt; and in its doubt, medieval culture did cling to one firm principle, one which was definitely *not* heretical. It was the double principle voiced by Augustine at the beginning of my lecture: that nature is unfathomable and that habit blinds us to this fact. As a guard against our own bad habits let me formulate that anew, and then finish. If there has been anything more conspicuous during the twentieth century than the prodigious discoveries of science, it is the absence of any sign that their pace is expected to slow up. That implies that the unsolved secrets of nature are infinite. Since the proportion of any two finite quantities to infinity are the same, that means we may as well know nothing. That may be too 'otherworldly' a conclusion. It may be only one side of the truth. But it *is* one side. And it is the side in whose presence, as we reflect our own burgeoning science, we gain most by consulting our great, great, great—twenty more of those—grandfathers, who looked out on what was basically the same world as ours but with, at their best, a clearer consciousness of how small they were.

NOTES

1. *De utilitate credendi*, c. 16, Migne, *Patrologia latina*, vol. 42, col. 90 (henceforth referred to in the form *Pat. lat.* 42.90). Commentary: A Van Hove, *La doctrine du miracle chez saint Thomas* (Paris 1927), pp. 26–38. The theme is echoed across a wide range of religious and didactic literature, e.g. Gregory the Great, *Hom. in evang.* 26, c.12 (*Pat. lat.* 76.1204); Guitmund of Aversa, *De corporis et sanguinis Christi veritate in Eucharistia*, III (*Pat. lat.* 149.1479A); Thomas von Zirclaria, *Der welhische Gast*, lines 9693–716, ed. H. Rückert (Quedlinburg 1852), p. 264.
2. See pp. 15–16 of Chapter 1 above.
3. An idea chronicled by H. de Lubac, *Surnaturel* (Paris 1946).
4. Bartholomeus Anglicus, *De proprietatibus rerum*, Bk. 15 c. 57 (Frankfurt 1601), p. 654: the environs of Paris are 'aere et flumine philosophantibus congruentes, camporum, pratorum et montium pulchritudine fessorum in studio oculos recreantes et reficientes'—it being apparently the intellectuals, then as later, who appreciated these things. Similar remarks abut the woodlands near Senlis were made in 1323 by the philosopher John of Jandun, *De laudibus Parisius*, Pt. 4, ed. A. J. V. Le Roux de Lincy and L. M. Tisserand, *Paris et ses historiens au XIVe et XVe siècles* (*Hist. générale de Paris*) (Paris 1867), pp. 32–78, on p. 76. Orientation: B. Bischoff, *Mittelalterliche Studien* (Stuttgart 1966–7), I, p. 22; II. p. 99; and at the two extremes of our period, D. S. W. Wallace Hadrill, *The greek patristic view of nature* (Manchester 1968), and K. Thomas, *Man and the natural world. Changing attitudes in England, 1500–1800* (London 1983), p. 407.
5. A. C. Crombie, 'Quantification in medieval physics', *Isis*, **52** (1961) 143–60 (reprinted three times, e.g. in S. Thrupp, ed., *Change in medieval society* (London 1965), pp. 188–207).
6. M.-D. Chenu, *La théologie au douzième siecle* (Paris 1966), pp. 19–51; translated by J. Taylor and L. K. Little as *Nature, man and society in the twelfth century* (Chicago, IL 1968), pp. 1–48.
7. T. Gregory, 'L'idea della Natura nella filosofia medioevale prima dell'ingresso della fisica di Aristotele', in *La filosofia della natura nel medioevo*. Atti del terzo congresso internazionale di filosofia medioevale, Passo della Mendola, 31 Aug–5 Sep 1964 (Milan 1966), pp. 27–65.
8. *The allegory of love* (Oxford 1936), c. 2, pp. 44–87.
9. William of Conches, *Dialogus de substantiis physicis* (*Dragmaticon*),

ed. G. Gratarolus (Strasbourg 1567), p. 31; quoted by T. Gregory, 'L'idea della Natura', p. 42 (see note 7), and T. Gregory, *Anima mundi. La filosofia di Guglielmo di Conches e la scuola di Chartres* (Florence 1955), p. 178.

10. *Abstract of the prospectus of a system of philosophy*, on the flyleaf of Spencer's *The classification of the sciences* (London 1864).
11. W. von den Steinen, *Der Kosmos des Mittelalters*, (2nd edn) (Bern 1967).
12. C. Erickson (New York 1976).
13. By H. O. Taylor, (4th edn) (New York 1925).
14. R. G. Collingwood, *The idea of nature* (Oxford 1945). Cf. 'The medieval view of nature', in W. J. Brandt, *The shape of medieval history* (New Haven 1966), pp. 1–42; and the title of the paper by Professor Gregory mentioned in note 7 above.
15. By C. S. Lewis (Cambridge 1964, often reprinted).
16. By E. M. W. Tillyard (London 1943).
17. See pp. 1–2 of Chapter 1 above.
18. *Vita sancti Norberti* ('B'), chapter 3, para 14, in *Acta sanctorum, 6 June* I, p. 824F: 'homines sensibus carnis dediti, et rebus corporeis assuefacti, nec rationem quaerunt, nec causam attendunt; existimantes omnia fortuitis et inopinatis motibus provenire'. Cf. A. Murray, *Reason and society in the Middle Ages* (Oxford 1978), p. 14, for other examples of this general doctrine.
19. E.g. Humbert de Romans, *De modo prompte cudendi sermones*, Bk. I, in M. de la Bigne, ed., *Maxima biblioteca veterum patrum* (Lyons 1677), Vol. 25, cols. 456E–567F.
20. Lines 92–3, ed. C.L. Wrenn (London 1953), p. 97: þaet sē Aelmihtiga eorðan worhte,/wlite-beorhtne wang, swā waeter bebūgeð. Dating: D. D. Short, *Beowulf scholarship* (New York 1980), p. 348. I do not exclude poetic license. It still does not flatter the audience.
21. Pliny, *Nat. Hist.* II, c. 65, ed. H. Rackham, Leob edition (Cambridge, MA 1949), Vol. 1, pp. 296–301; Manilius, *Astronomica*, I, lines 650 –2, 231 and 219–20, ed. G. P. Goold, Loeb edition (Cambridge, MA 1977), pp. 56–7, 20–23; Hyginus, *De astronomia*, I, 8, para 1, ed. A. Le Boeuffle, Collection des Universités de France (Paris 1983), p. 12; Isidore, *De natura rerum*, c. 48 (i), ed. J. Fontaine, Bibliothèque de l'Ecole des Hautes Etudes Hispaniques, 28 (Bordeaux 1960), p. 325. 5–6; *Etymologiae*, III, xix, 1, ed. W. M. Lindsay (Oxford 1911); Bede, *De natura rerum*, c. 46, ed. C. W. Jones (Turnhout 1975), pp. 228–9.
22. P. H. Blair, *The world of Bede* (London 1970), p. 261; Brandt p.10 n. 28 (see note 14).

23. 'Nostrates ... incredibili pavore exterriti, nichil aliud quam diem iuditii putant imminere ... hanc alienam rutilantibus stellis noctem in tantum expavit, ut incredibili anxietate diversas quasi tutandae vitae exquireret latebras. Sic alii vasis vinariis, alii cistis, alii sub carris turpiter sese recondunt, quisque pro lucro vitae computat si quod pro hac inusitata nocte sibi reperire queat latibulum.' Anselm, *Gesta episcoporum Tungrensium, Trajectensium et Leodicensium*, c. 24, *Mon. Germ. Hist., Scriptores*, 7, p. 202, lines 12–24. Anselm's account is based on an eye-witness report by Bishop Wazo of Liège, successor to the hero of the story, Evraclus. Cf. the complementary narrative in Reiner's *Vita Evracli Leodicensi episcopi*, c. 7, in *Mon. Germ. Hist., Scriptores*, 20, p. 563 col. A; and, for the eclipse, D. Justin Schove and A. Fletcher, *Chronology of eclipse and comets, A.D. 1–1000* (London 1984), p. 235. At the battle of Zamora on 19 July 939 a total solar eclipse had similarly caused 'the minds of the young and inexperienced' to be 'much troubled'; J. A. Condé, *The Arabs in Spain*, Vol. I (Madrid 1820; English trans., London 1837), p. 424, quoting an Arabic source; cf. Schove and Fletcher, pp. 226–8. Radulfus Glaber's *Historiae* include further examples, e.g. Bk. 5, c. 2, para. 18, ed. J. France (Oxford 1989), p. 242: 'insulsum enim vulgus perhibet stellam de celo cadere'. Cf. St. Thomas Aquinas, *Summa theologica*, I, 105 a.7, resp: 'eclipsim solis miratur rusticus, non autem astrologus'.
24. E. Le Roy Ladurie, *Montaillou, village occitan de 1294 à 1324* (Paris 1975), c. 2, pp. 69–73.
25. *Miracula sancti Benedicti*, Bk. V. c. 12, ed. E. de Certain, Societé pour l'Histoire de France (Paris 1858), p. 210.
26. A.J. Gurevich, *Categories of medieval culture*, trans. G. L. Campbell (London 1985), c.3, esp. pp. 45–6. Arithmetic: Murray, pp. 141–61, 'The dark age of arithmetic' (see note 18); Le Roy Ladurie, pp. 424–31, esp. 430 (see note 24); cf. C. Lévi-Strauss, *The savage mind*, (London 1966), esp. pp. 233–69.
27. Guilelmus Alvernus, *De legibus*, c. 26, *Opera omnia* (Paris 1674), pp. 81bA–83aA.
28. For instance, R. Bartlett, *Trial by fire and water: the medieval judicial ordeal* (Oxford 1986). Cf. C. Plummer, ed., *Vitae sanctorum Hiberniae*, 2 volumes (Oxford 1910), Vol. 1, Introduction, pp. cxxxiii–cxli and cxlvi–clvii. Water, unprepared by any of the formalities of the ordeal, rejects a murderer as impure in A. Bausch, ed., *Ein bayerisches Mirakelbuch aus de Karolingerzeit. Die Moheimer Walpurgiswunder des Priestes Wolfrad* (Regensburg 1979), p. 230, lines 26–9.

29. J. de Vries, *Altgermanische Religionsgeschichte*, 2 volumes (2nd edn) (Berlin 1956–7), esp. paras. 245–51, pp. 344–54; effect of migration, L. Musset, 'La pénétration chrétienne dans l'Europe du nord et son influence sur la civilisation scandinave', in *La conversione al cristianesimo nell'Europa dell'alto medioevo*, Settimane di studio sul alto medioevo, 14 (Spoleto 1967), pp. 263–326, esp. pp. 264–5. V. I. J. Flint, *The rise of magic in early medieval Europe* (Princeton, NJ 1991), pp. 442 (demons), 450 (springs).
30. P. Browe, *Die eucharistischen Wunder des Mittelalters* (Breslau 1938).
31. The main series, *Studien zur Naturphilosophie der Spätscholastik*, was published in Rome between 1951 and 1958 in successive volumes of the collection 'Storia e letteratura'. Scholastic conservation of multiple opinions is the subject of a long chapter by J. Pelikan in his *The Christian tradition*, Vol. 4 (Chicago, IL 1984), pp. 10–68.
32. For the following: E. Grant, 'Cosmology', and O. Pedersen, 'Astronomy', in D.C. Lindberg, *Science in the Middle Ages* (Chicago, IL 1978), esp. pp. 280–4 and 320–9.
33. L. Thorndike, 'Astronomical observations made at Paris from 1312 to 1315', *Isis*, **38** (1947–8) 200–5.
34. The most accessible histories of Neoplatonism are A. H. Armstrong, ed., *The Cambridge history of later Greek and early medieval philosophy* (Cambridge 1967); and R. T. Wallis, *Neoplatonism* (London 1972).
35. F. Van Steenberghen, *La philosophie au XIIIe siècle* (Louvain 1966), p. 591; D. S. Rice, 'Medieval Harran', *Anatolian Studies*, **2** (1952) 36–83; R. Lemay, *Abu Ma'shar and Latin Aristotelianism in the twelfth century* (Beirut 1962), pp. 374–5.
36. H. Denifle and F. Ehrle, *Archiv für Literatur-und Kirchengeschichte des Mittelalters*, **6** (Freiburg 1889) 563; G. R. Galbraith, *The constitution of the Dominican order* (Manchester 1925), p.176.
37. S. C. McCluskey, 'Gregory of Tours, monastic timekeeping, and early Christian attitudes to astronomy', *Isis*, **81** (1990) 8–22.
38. E. J. Dijksterhuis, *The mechanization of the world picture*, trans. C. Dikshoorn (Oxford 1961), pp. 180–1; other examples of theological material in physical discusson, ibid., pp. 179–90; and A. Maier, *Zwischen Philosophie und Mechanik* (Rome 1958), p. 48 (Antichrist as an example of *ens in potentia*). The feature is also noticed by Crombie, 'Quantification' pp. 151, 154–5 (ed. Thrupp, pp. 196, 201), (see note 5).
39. R. W. Southern, *Robert Grosseteste* (Oxford 1986), esp. pp. 219–23.
40. Gregory, *Anima mundi*, p. 43 and n.4; p. 107 (see note 9). Additions,

showing the extent of familiarity with this text and its application: *Praedicatio Goliae* in T. Wright, *Latin poems* (London 1841), p. 32, lines 31–8; Henry of Ghent, *Summae questionum ordinarium*, art. xi, qu. vii, ed. Jodocus Badius Ascensius (Paris 1520), fol. 82vc.

41. H.-I. Marrou, *Saint Augustin et la fin de la culture antique* (Paris 1938–49), pp. 331–413.
42. Chapter 15 (ii), ed. R. Roques and others, *Denys l'Aréopagite, La hiérarchie céleste*, Sources chrétiennes 58 (Paris 1958), pp. 169–71; cf. *Pat. lat.* 122, 1065–1066A (Erigena's Latin version). Medieval influence: J. Leclercq, F. Vandenbroucke, and L. Bouyer, *La spiritualité du moyen âge*, Histoire de la spiritualité chrétienne, II (Paris 1961), p. 701.
43. Ibid., pp. 285–6, 404. The legend: T. Graesse, ed., *Jacobi a Voragine legenda aurea* (Dresden 1846), c. 153 (148), (pp. 680–686); F. S. Ellis, ed., *The golden legend . . . as Englished by William Caxton* (London 1922), Vol. 5, pp. 244–55.
44. J. M. Parent, *La doctrine de la Création à l'école de Chartres* (Paris 1938); Gregory, *Anima mundi* pp. 175–201 (see note 9).
45. Gregory, ibid., and more specifically in 'L'idea di Natura' (see note 7); developed by G. D. Economou, *The goddess Natura in medieval literature* (Cambridge, MA 1972), p. 213.
46. *Chartularium universitatis parisiensis*, ed. H. Denifle, Vol. 1 (Paris 1889), p. 544 (No. 3). Cf. pp. 546 (No. 56) and 547 (No. 63).
47. Cambridge, MA 1936. Lovejoy argued that there was a 'conflict' in medieval treatment of his idea (c. 2, pp. 67–98), and especially (pp. 82–4) between the remote and intimate ideas of God. Of course there was. Psalm 112 says as much. It is a flaw in Lovejoy's classic that he overlooks the centrality of this apparent paradox in the Semitic idea of God.
48. The controversy in outline: E. Gilson, *Saint Thomas Aquinas*, Annual Lecture on a Master Mind, *Proceedings of the British Academy*, **21** (London 1935).
49. F. Van Steenberghen, *Aristotle in the west* (Louvain 1955), esp. pp. 66–77.
50. F. Van Steenberghen, 'La controverse sur l'éternité du monde au XIIIe siècle', in that author's *Introduction à l'étude de la philosophie médiévale* (Louvain 1974), pp. 512–30. My remarks on Aristotle's cast of mind, in these respects, are indebted to its brilliant exposition by F. Brunner, *Platonisme et Aristotélisme: la critique d'Ibn Gabirol par St. Thomas d'Aquin*. Chaire Cardinal Mercier 1963, No. 2 (Louvain 1965), pp. 7–32.

51. Quantity and quality: R. Aigrain, *L'hagiographie* (Paris 1953).
52. A thesis restated by Flint, *The rise of magic* (see note 29).
53. The conclusion is drawn on the heretics' behalf by their critic Salvo Burci of Piacenza in *Liber supra Stella*, in Cod. Flor. Laurent. Mugell. 12, fols. 66va–68vb (a section not in any of the printed versions), cf. A. Borst, *Die Katharer* (Stuttgart 1953), p. 329 and I. von Döllinger, *Beiträge zur Sektengeschichte des Mittelalters* (Munich 1890), 2, pp. 52–85. Similar testimony to the Cathars' denial of physical miracles in Anselm of Alexandria, *Tractatus de haereticis*, ed. A. Dondaine, *Archivum fratrum praedicatorum*, **20** (1950) 310–11, and *Brevis summula contra errores haereticorum* ed. C. Douais, quoted by Borst, p. 166 n.18 (a note which also cites evidence of the heretics' inconsistency in this regard).
54. *De utilitate credendi*, c. 16, quoted by Van Hove, *La doctrine du miracle*, p. 29 (see note 1).
55. Van Hove, p. 42 (Alexander of Hales); more generally pp.10–14, 16, 40–6; and for Aquinas and natural laws, pp. 67–72 (see note 1). De Lubac, pp. 325–428 (see note 3). Some key passages: Thomas Aquinas, *Summa theologica* I, 105, 7; and *De potentia* 6, 2 obj. corp. ad 1, 2 and 4.
56. Scepticism: K. Michalski, *La philosophie au XIVe siècle: six études*, ed. K. Flasch. Opuscula philosophica, 1 (Frankfurt 1969); J. R. Weinberg, *Nicholas of Autrecourt* (Princeton 1948). Summary of later discussion: A. Michel, 'Miracle', in A. Vacant, ed., *Dictionnaire de théologie catholique*, Vol. 10 (Paris 1928), cols. 1798–859; at cols. 1812–33.
57. L. Thorndike, *A history of magic and experimental science*, Vol. 2 (New York 1923), supplemented by L. Delisle, 'Traités divers sur les propriétés des choses', *Histoire littéraire de la France*, Vol. 30 (Paris 1888), pp. 334–388.
58. E.g. Guilelmus Alvernus, *De universo*, I, c. 11 (edn. of Venice 1591, pp. 571–3); Bernardus Silvester, *Megacosmos*, ed. C. S. Barach and J. Wrobel (Frankfurt am Main 1876), pp. 10.52, 6.25–33, 20.161–6, 21.205–10, 30.51–4; Ristoro de Arezzo, *La composizione del Mondo*, ed. A. Morino (Florence 1976), p. 251 (but there is scarcely any page of this last work which does not illustrate the thesis defended here).
59. Guilelmus Alvernus, *De universo*, Part I, c. 21, *Opera omnia* (Paris 1674), p. 615bCD.
60. Van Hove, pp. 13–18 (see note 1); Gregory, *Anima mundi*, pp. 180–1 (see note 9); R. Markus, 'Augustine: God and nature', in Armstrong pp. 398–402 (see note 34).

61. Among growing-pains I mean especially the difficulty, à la Alice-in-Wonderland, of understanding that negative words do not refer to anything. Examples are *nihil*, D. P. Henry, 'Predictables and categories', in N. Kretzmann and others. *The Cambridge history of later medieval philosophy* (Cambridge 1982), pp. 128–42; p. 142 (quoting Anselm, *Monologion*, c. 19); *nullus*, K. Michalski, 'Le criticisme et le scepticisme dans la philosophie du XIVe siècle', *Bulletin international de l'Académie polonaise des sciences et des lettres. Classe de philologie, classe d'histoire et de philosophie* (Cracow 1925), p. 59 (r.p. in the work quoted in note 56, pp. 67–149); silence and darkness, see the passage from Chalcidius quoted by Gregory, *Anima mundi* p. 194, n.1 (see note 9); the void, E. J. Dijksterhuis, *The mechanization of the world-picture* (Oxford 1961), pp. 142–5; and finally 'St. Nemo', in P. Lehmann, *Die Parödie im Mittelalter* (Munich 1922), pp. 240–6.
62. Generally on hylemorphism: D. Ross, *Aristotle* (5th edn) (Oxford 1949), pp. 63–75, 167–76. Of its centrality in thirteenth-century thought and the problems posed by change: R. Zavalloni, *Richard de Mediavilla et la controverse sur la pluralité des formes* (Louvain 1951), pp. 248, 280 (and nn. 59–60), 475–503.
63. Both stages well depicted by P. Boyde, *Dante philomythes and philosopher* (Cambridge 1981), pp. 57–111.
64. Cardinal winds: e.g. Isidore, *De natura rerum*, c. 37 (p. 295) (see note 21); T. Silverstein, ed., 'Liber Hermetis Mercurii triplicis de VI rerum principiis', *Archives d'histoire doctrinale et littéraire du moyen âge*, 30 (Paris 1955), pp. 217–301, p. 272. The emergence of the arithmetical mentality: Murray, *Reason and society*, pp. 162–87 (see note 18).
65. E. Zilsel, 'The genesis of the concept of physical law', *The Philosophical Review*, **51** (1942) 245–79, fails the medieval period, while Crombie, pp. 147–8 (ed. Thrupp, p. 193) (see note 5) finds the term 'natural laws' first in Roger Bacon. But the term *lex*, used in a natural context, was part of an ancient inheritance familiar to the few who drew from it, as for instance in Atto of Vercelli, whose sermon on the nature of astral influence (No. 3, Octave of Christmas) says 'hanc illis legem Creator omnium in principio posuit . . .' (*Pat. lat.* 134.837A).
66. Van Hove, pp. 75–80, quoting *Summa contra gentiles*, 2, c. 29 (see note 1).
67. E.g. Peter Damian, *De divina omnipotentia*, cc. 10–11 (*Pat. lat.* 145, 612C–3A); Thomas Aquinas, *De potentia* q.6, a.2, ad 8. Cf. Van Hove, pp. 86–90; another eleventh-century view (Manegold of Lautenbach) in Gregory 'L'idea', p. 36 (see note 7), and the remarks of Dijksterhuis, p. 152–3 (see note 38).

3

The scientific revolution of the seventeenth century: the construction of a new world view

RICHARD S. WESTFALL

The invitation to expound the seventeenth century's conception of nature led me initially to ponder a somewhat different question of my own: the essence of the scientific revolution. As I understand the issue, the answer to my question is identical with the answer to yours.

The idea that there was a scientific revolution in the seventeenth century has been around for a long time, and no one of whom I know seriously contends that we can dispense with the notion.[1] Major changes did take place in the scientific enterprise during the seventeenth century, and the word 'revolution' does not seem to exaggerate their importance. About the nature of the changes, however, there is anything but agreement. For some the level of scientific activity itself is an essential feature, and they look for the factors, such as the Puritan ethic, that legitimated the study of nature.[2] For others the critical element is social; in every instance with which I am familiar, the rise of a capitalistic economy and the encouragement it offered to certain kinds of knowledge play a central role in this interpretation[3] The alliance of science with technology naturally forms an important aspect of this interpretation.[4]

If it is the essence of the scientific revolution we wish to explore—that feature which constituted an epoch in the study of nature—I think convincing arguments can be deployed against these interpretations. The study of nature had always been a distinguishing feature of Western Civilization. One could not begin adequately to describe the Greek world without it. Medieval Europe revived Aristotle's philosophy; in its universities it made Aristotelian natural philosophy the core of the arts curriculum, and to pursue it called into being a scientific community more extensive by far than any previous civilization had known. It is far from evident that the study of nature was in need of legitimation in the seventeenth century.[5] The argument about capitalism appears to me to project the experience of the nineteenth and twentieth centuries back onto the seventeenth without carefully examining how well it fits the realities of the earlier age. With a few exceptions, it was not capitalists who patronized and fostered scientific study during the seventeenth century. With fewer exceptions, the products of seventeenth-century science had little relevance to seventeenth-century capitalism. If there were distinct areas in which scientific study found application to technology during the seventeenth century, this was hardly an innovation, for the most important of these areas had known the relation of science to utility well before the scientific revolution. Medicine and pharmacology come immediately to mind, and to them one can add such fields as navigation, cartography, military engineering, and water management. Easily the most important new technological enterprise associated with science in the seventeenth century was the construction of scientific instruments. Science itself was the beneficiary of this application of scientific knowledge, though a new industry, which was undoubtedly capitalistic, did emerge from it.

What made the scientific revolution revoluntionary? None of the above in my opinion. Neither was it any specific discovery or theory. Rather it was the new view of physical reality, the new conception of nature, which constituted the epoch. During the seventeenth century scientists came to look upon the world in which we live in a way radically different from anything the world had ever known before. With a couple of prominent exceptions, they did not set out consciously to construct a new conception of nature, but the new conception that the community of scientists as a whole elaborated furnished the framework within which specific discoveries were possible and within which they acquired meaning. Though much has been added to it during the intervening three hundred years and many details changed, the seventeenth-century conception of nature has remained the basis of the Western view of reality ever since, so that it is impossible to imagine the whole enterprise of modern science, the central and determining feature of contemporary Western Civilization, apart from this background. If I can refer to the combined achievement of a number of men spread over more than a hundred years as an event, it seems clear to me that there have been few other events of Western history that can rival the elaboration of the new conception of nature in importance.

My assigned function, however, is not to argue its significance but to expound the seventeenth-century conception of nature. Without further digression, let me turn to it. I suggest that we need four headings to describe the conception of nature adequately. During the scientific revolution nature was quantified; it was mechanized; it was perceived to be other; it was secularized.

To say that nature was quantified during the scientific revolution is not, I am well aware, to say anything new. Over fifty years ago E. A. Burtt made the centrality of mathematics in the new conception of nature the theme of his influential *Metaphysical foundations of modern physical science*, and a decade later Alexandre Koyré coined the phrase, the geometrization of nature, to emphasize the critical importance of the same feature.[6] Well known and much repeated statements from the age express the new outlook.

> Geometry [said Kepler], being part of the divine mind from time immemorial, from before the origin of things being God Himself (for what is in God that is not God Himself?), has supplied God with the models for the creation of the world and has been transferred to man together with the image of God. Geometry was not received inside through the eyes.[7]

Galileo said much the same thing in different words.

> Philosophy is written in this grand book, the universe, which stands continually open to our gaze. But the book cannot be understood unless one first learns to comprehend the language and read the letters in which it is composed. It is written in the language of mathematics, and its characters are triangles, circles, and other geometric figures without which it is humanly impossible to understand a single word of it.[8]

The geometrization of nature implied measurability, and it found expression, not only in abstract statements of metaphysical principles, but also in practical measurements. It is relevant to this theme to note that when the seventeenth century dawned there were not many quantities that scientists could measure with accuracy. Because of the economic importance of the precious metals, they had precision balances on which to weigh. They had measuring rods with divisions as fine as the eye could easily distinguish for linear dimensions. The instruments of Tycho Brahe had recently made it possible to measure celestial angles to minutes where before astronomers had stopped at sixths of a degree. In themselves, Tycho's instruments illustrate the change I am describing, for there was nothing about the instruments that could not have been achieved centuries before. Only during the early phase of the scientific revolution had it begun to seem significant to design and build such devices. Beyond these three, weight, distance, and celestial angles, science was unable to measure anything except in crude terms. This applies to the important dimension of time, for example. Scientists could not measure many quantities that seem fundamental to us at all, and they seldom bothered to measure those they could.

I cite as an example of the world view about to be replaced, a commentary on Aristotle's *De caelo* compiled by Galileo for his personal use in the late 1580s. Since I intend to draw upon this manuscript, which expounds a number of questions in Scholastic natural philosophy, several times, I need to discuss it briefly. When the manuscript was published in the National Edition of Galileo's works at the turn of the century, it appeared under the heading 'Juvenilia'.[9] As a result of outstanding recent scholarship, the most important contemporary contribution to the understanding of Galileo, we have learned that the overwhelming proportion of the manuscript was copied verbatim from lecture notes of professors at the Jesuit Collegio Romano, and because we know when specific professors taught, we have realized that the manuscript was not at all a juvenile exercise but the work of a mature if still young professor at the University of Pisa who was consolidating his knowledge of natural philosophy.[10] Latin verbs in the first person singular appear frequently in it, but even though the manuscript probably represents Galileo's own views on natural philosophy when he was about twenty-five years old, we cannot identify the implied personal pronoun with Galileo. He copied the verbs along with the rest from the Jesuit professors, who in turn drew upon a tradition of natural philosophy at that time well over three hundred years old. I interpret the pronoun to refer then to some ideal Scholastic philosopher, and I will treat the manuscript as an exposition of the conception of nature that the scientific revolution replaced. Do not imagine that in discussing it I intend to cast scorn on Scholastic natural philosophy. We have also learned of late, and continue to learn, what an important and creative tradition in the study of nature it was. I insist only that it differed from seventeenth-century science.

The important feature of the manuscript for my present purpose is the absence of quantitative elements in it. It proceeds by verbal discussion instead of numerical calculations, and the conception of nature it presents is correspondingly qualitative. At one point, it is true, our ideal Scholastic philosopher states that the maximum intensity of a quality is eight degrees, and at another that the maximum intensity of heat is eight degrees.[11] Do not be deceived. The number does not correspond to any instrument or operation by which the author might undertake to measure some specific quality such as temperature. It is just a way of talking about qualities, another dimension of the qualitative Scholastic philosophy which pursued a set of questions wholly different from those of seventeenth century science.

As a manuscript in the hand of Galileo the commentary is even more arresting, for it was Galileo who would later, in his *Two new sciences*, establish a quantitative science of kinematics, which became the cornerstone of the whole structure of modern quantitative science. The features of Galileo's science of mechanics are well known, however, and despite its quantitative nature his kinematics does not in fact contain many more measurements than the manuscript commentary on *De caelo*.

Half a century after Galileo, however, the new spirit he helped to create was spreading beyond the physical sciences even into the life sciences and raising new questions in every field it touched. Around 1670 Antoni van Leeuwenhoek began to make microscopes and to examine, as the first human being ever to see them, various protozoa, bacteria, and other microscopic forms of life. Almost his first impulse was to measure the creatures he had discovered. Virtually every one of the letters he wrote to the Royal Society, his primary form of publication, had numbers in it. Thus he described one sort of 'little animals' as 'more than a thousand times smaller than the eye of a full-grown Louse ...'[12] When Leeuwenhoek spoke of size, he usually referred to volume, as he did here; he was saying then that the little animals in question were less than one tenth of the eye of a louse in length. He had seen smaller ones. In an infusion of pepper he found creatures that he estimated to number more than six or eight thousand in a drop of water.[13] Others were smaller than these; he was willing to claim there were 100000 of them in a drop of water.[14] Two years later he was seeing creatures he judged to number 30000000 in a drop the size of a coarse grain of sand.[15]

Not surprisingly, voices of disbelief were raised in the Royal Society when they heard descriptions of living beings smaller than anything anyone had even dreamed of before. What the fellows of the Society learned was that Leeuwenhoek's numbers had not appeared merely as vague guesses. Because it seemed important to him to know the size of these creatures accurately, he invented what he called his 'counter', a capillary tube into which he sucked up a quantity of water about as large as a grain of millet. He divided the capillary into 25 or 30 or more parts, counted the number of little animals in a single part, and arrived at some of his total numbers by multiplication.[16] He also developed a scale of dimensions that started with a fine grain of sand, the diameter of which he measured initially as one-eightieth of an inch, and later as one-hundredth. Some of his little animals appeared to be one-twelfth the grain of sand in diameter, another type one-fifth of these, and a third type one-tenth the second.[17] By employing this scale, he was able to estimate the sizes of creatures only one-sixty-thousandth of an inch across. Modern students of biology, who can identify the species in question from Leeuwenhoek's descriptions and drawings of them, have not been reluctant to take his scale seriously in order to compare his measurements with their own. They find, of course, that Leeuwenhoek's were not precisely accurate, but invariably they had the right order of magnitude, and the great majority fell within twenty-five per cent of the absolute values deemed correct today. They were in fact valid exercises in quantitative science.

Indeed, Leeuwenhoek was not the first scientist who brought measurement into the realm of the microscopic. A few years earlier Isaac Newton had read Robert Hooke's *Micrographia* and found there an optical phenomenon that involved similar magnitudes, the colours in thin transparent films.[18] A little before Leeuwenhoek constructed his first microscopes, Newton started to measure what Hooke had been able only to describe. His device was a lens of known curvature pressed down on a flat sheet of glass to create a thin film of air between the two. When he looked down on the lens from above, he saw the familiar pattern of concentric circles that we still call Newton's rings—a dark spot in the centre surrounded by a series of about six dark rings, where the film was of such thickness that it transmitted light, and between the dark rings bright ones coloured with the hues of the rainbow, where the film reflected light to his eye. From the measured diameters he could calculate the thickness of film that corresponded to each ring.[19]

Like Leeuwenhoek, Newton did not care to deal in more-or-less. He wanted quantitative precision. Using a set of pointers, he measured the diameters of rings, not just to hundredths of an inch, but to fractions of a hundredth. Thus one experiment records the following set of diameters: 23 1/2, 34 1/3, 42 1/3, 49, 54 3/4, 60. Recall that these measurements were mankind's first attempt to deal with magnitudes of the order of his films; there was no established body of data from which he could have copied or calculated the measurements. Nevertheless, we cannot avoid asking, as the Royal Society did of Leeuwenhoek, whether Newton was deluding himself with such figures. The question is difficult to answer because we have to make arbitrary choices about what wavelengths to compare with his dark and bright circles. There are limits to our arbitrary choices, however, and they do not extend far enough to bring Newton's measurements into agreement with modern data. The thicknesses of films that he calculated were apparently about ten per cent too large.

It would be misleading to leave the matter there, however. His error was not random but systematic, and must therefore have flowed from a source common to all the measurements, probably his determination of the curvature of the lens. When we look at another aspect of these experiments, the periodicity of the rings, the degree of precision looks much better, for here the curvature of the lens, being common to all the measurements in a set, cancels out. In Newton's experimental arrangement, the thickness of the film varies as the square of the diameter of the rings. What he did was to square the measured diameters and subtract each square from the next. If the differences of the squares are constant, then the squares and the thicknesses of film corresponding to them form an arithmetic series, demonstrating that the phenomena are periodic; that is, the addition of equal increments of thickness causes the same optical phenomena to reappear. In the set of measurements quoted above, the differences of squares were 626, 613, 609, 596, 603.[20] The degree of precision enabled Newton to track down a consistent divergence that appeared between sets of measurements and to establish that one face of the lens ('wch hath ye 5 little short scratches together') had a shorter radius of curvature than the other. The difference in curvature, as he calculated it, corresponded to a difference of less than one hundredth of an inch in the diameter of the innermost ring and about two hundredths of an inch in the diameter of the sixth. Newton had found the concept of periodicity in Hooke, but it was these experiments which first demonstrated the periodicity of an optical phenomenon. Quantitative precision was the heart of the demonstration.

Already a few years earlier, as he neared the end of his undergraduate studies, Newton had carried out another significant measurement of a different sort. At that time he had just discovered the new science. Among other books that he read was the English translation of Galileo's *Dialogue*, and in it he found Galileo's imperfect reply to one of the standard objections against the Copernican system, to wit, that the centrifugal force of a spinning earth would hurl loose bodies into space.[21] The objection had been argued pro and con for a century by then; Newton saw at once that it was merely a problem in quantitative physics that could be settled definitely by measurement and calculation.

Galileo offered a figure for the acceleration of gravity. Newton could calculate the centrifugal acceleration from the known size of the earth and its rate of rotation. One had only to compare the two quantities, both of which depended on empirical measurements.

In fact the problem was more difficult than he first thought. As far as Newton was aware, no one had analysed the strength of the forces in circular motion, and the simple concepts he initially employed were misleading. Never mind; he quickly recognized their inadequacy and replaced them with an analysis quantitatively identical with the one we still use.[22] Eventually a central part of his science of dynamics, the analysis by itself displays the new approach to nature. With it Newton arrived at the conclusion that the acceleration of gravity is 150 times greater than the centrifugal acceleration from the earth's rotation. As far as the original problem was concerned, the calculation demonstrated that loose objects will not be thrown off a turning earth.[23]

What interests me today, however, is the other half of the manuscript, in which Newton checked Galileo's measurement of the acceleration of gravity. For his analysis of circular motion led him to realize that he could use a conical pendulum for that purpose. What Newton did was to measure the periods of two different simple pendulums, which he converted in thought to conical pendulums of the same vertical heights and periods, and from the imagined conical pendulums, using his analysis of circular motion and comparing its outward thrust with the downward thrust of gravity on the bob, he calculated the distance a body would fall from rest in a second, in effect, $g/2$. The problem was to measure the periods. The sun was the only accurate chronometer available; Newton had been a sun-dialer from his youth. The manuscript contains peculiar ratios. First,

$$7/54 = 56/x$$

that is, seven units of some sort correspond to one eighth of an hour, and these seven units taken together contain fifty-four smaller units, of which an hour then corresponds to 432 ($432 = x$). A second ratio states that

$$6/21 = 432/y.$$

Twenty-one oscillations of the pendulum are completed in six of the smaller units; 1512 oscillations ($1512 = y$) would then be completed in one hour. 1512 is the number Newton used to compute the period.[24]

I have been willing to speculate on what these peculiar ratios could have referred to, but the facts in the manuscript are not called into question by the uncertainty of my speculations.[25] That is, the manuscript records Newton's success in measuring intervals of about fifty seconds (six of the smaller units) with sufficient accuracy to calculate the periods of two different pendulums to within one per cent of the figures we would arrive at starting with our well-established value of g. The undergraduate was confident enough in his procedure, I might add, to accept his own consequent computation of $g/2$, even though it was almost exactly twice the one he found in Galileo. As far as the Copernican problem is concerned, gravity had now been shown to be 300 times greater than the centrifugal force from the earth's rotation. It is, however, the measurement itself that I wish to insist on here. If you want to understand one of the essential features of the new conception of nature, you cannot contemplate too fully the meaning of the three measurements I have just described. The world had never seen anything like them before.

Quantity was not the only feature of the new conception; the seventeenth century also mechanized nature. In no part of its new approach to nature was the age more fully self-conscious. Early in the century Descartes's education convinced him that mankind's entire philosophic tradition had not managed to settle any question at all; as he put it, 'there is nothing imaginable so strange or so little credible that it has not been maintained by one philosopher or other . . .'[26] He determined then to purge his mind of all the uncertainty of the past in order that he might restock it only with opinions that reason had certified. Almost the first thing that went, as Descartes began his program of systematic doubt, was not merely the established conception of nature, but nature itself. Our belief in the existence of a world external to ourselves has rested on the evidence of the senses. But everyone knows that the senses sometimes err. The existence of the external world cannot then be certain beyond possible doubt. Before he was done, of course, Descartes restored the existence of nature, now as a demonstrated truth instead of an unexamined assumption but the nature he restored to existence was, as I implied, different by conscious choice from the one he had rejected. Shorn of any source of spontaneous activity, it was a world of passive matter, divided of necessity into separate particles, which moved where the impact of other particles forced them to move.

Though Descartes was the most significant influence in the development of this aspect of the new conception, there were other philosophers of his generation who drew upon the same sources of ancient atomism and arrived at similar conclusions. Pierre Gassendi and Thomas Hobbes are the best known among them. Robert Boyle insisted that the opinions all of them shared about physical reality far outweighed those on which they differed, and he coined the name 'mechanical philosophy' to describe the new view. He also popularized the image of the clock to characterize nature, which was conceived by the new school as a great machine.[27]

Again compare this idea of nature with that found in Galileo's manuscript. It is not just that our ideal Scholastic philosopher presented an organic rather than a mechanical view; the very questions that he posed could not have been answered in any relevant way in mechanical terms. As one example I cite a passage from the manuscript that fascinates me. The author was examining the concept that for every species there is a limit in size. Note already the taxonomic frame of reference, which invites analysis that deals in formal and final rather than efficient causes. Suppose that we have a horse as big as a horse can be, and that its owner in fury flogs it so that it swells. Is it still a horse? Having posed a good Scholastic question, our philosopher solved it in a good Scholastic manner with a logical distinction. Limits by way of corruption are external rather than internal; since the swelling would be a result of corruption, the beast, however abused, would at least still be a horse.[28]

In anything that one wishes to call science, questions such as that had disappeared by the middle of the seventeenth century. The issues posed by the barometer were answered in terms of pressures in equilibrium. To explain the phenomena of magnetism Descartes described streams of tiny screw-shaped particles that move through the screw-shaped pores in iron, left-hand threads for one pole and right-hand threads for the other, thus proving by example that there is indeed nothing imaginable so strange or so little credible that it has not been maintained by one philosopher or other. Different material effluvia explained the phenomena of static electricity. Light, the least obviously mechanical of the phenomena of physical nature, became for mechanical philosophers either corpuscles that move at immense velocities or pulses of motion transmitted through a material medium. The concept of the vortex, a huge whirlpool of matter that carries the planets in the same direction in the same plane about the sun, was not just a physical foundation for the Copernican theory, which every mechanical philosopher accepted as an essential aspect of the new view of nature. The vortex was also the perfect embodiment of the principles their philosophy sought to expound. The mechanical philosophers of the seventeenth century explained all the phenomena of nature by sole recourse to what Boyle called the two grand principles, particles of matter and motion.

Physical nature, however, yielded to mechanical explication with relative ease. Perhaps it was in its approach to living organisms that the new conception revealed itself most clearly. Where before physical nature had been conceived in terms suitable to the organic, now life was reduced to particles of matter in motion. Again Descartes set the tone. In his treatise on man, the second part of *The world*, he described a machine that performed all the physiological functions of a human being—circulation, digestion, nourishment and growth, perception, everything but rational thought.

> I desire you to consider [he concluded], that all these functions imitate those of a real man as perfectly as possible and that they follow naturally in this machine entirely from the disposition of the organs—no more nor less than do the movements of a clock or other automaton, from the arrangement of its counterweights and wheels. Wherefore it is not necessary, on their account, to conceive of any vegetative or sensitive soul in the machine, or any other principle of movement and life than its blood and its spirits, agitated by the heat of the fire which burns continually in its heart and is of no other nature than all those fires that occur in inanimate bodies.[29]

By the second half of the century, Descartes's assertion had become the prevailing orthodoxy among an influential segment of the life scientists. Consider John Mayow, whose experiments and essays showing that the same principle in air, which he called (among other names) the nitro-aerial spirit, sustains both combustion and animal life were once hailed as the virtual discovery of oxygen. Although no one maintains that exaggerated view any more, neither are historians inclined to dismiss the work that he and others did on the function of respiration. As it appears to me, Mayow's nitro-aerial spirit was the reincarnation of a Paracelsian active principle. It explained the corrosive activity of nitric acid, the elastic force of air, the explosive power of gunpowder, and the shattering energy of lightning. Above all, it explained the phenomena of life—the growth of plants, the capacity of muscles to move, the sustenance of animal life. But what matters to me here, Mayow, who did not eschew the language of activity, nevertheless also presented the aerial spirit as particles of given size and shape that interact in a mechanical fashion with other particles.[30] The mechanical philosophy was capable of translating any theory into the idiom of particles in motion. Mayow followed the predilections of the age when he expressed the concept of an active principle in those terms.

At much the same time, the Italian scientist Giovanni Alfonso Borelli analysed the motion of animals by treating the bones as levers and the muscles as forces. Borelli argued that every muscle acts at a pronounced mechanical disadvantage. The muscle itself is connected to the bone close to the joint that functions as the lever's fulcrum, while the load the muscle must move is always farther from the joint. Thus he added up the exertions required for a crouching man to pull himself up to a standing position and concluded that the man must exert a force four hundred and twenty times as great as his weight. Extending the argument in a manner which does not bear close examination, he concluded further that the man must exert a force seven times greater yet, or nearly three thousand times his weight, in order to continue the motion and leap into the air.[31] Borelli's student, Lorenzo Bellini, expanded the mechanistic analysis of motion into a fully fledged mechanistic physiology which drew heavily on Harvey's discovery of the circulation of the blood, and argued that disease is a result of impaired circulation.[32]

In Scotland, Archibald Pitcairne saw such doctrines if he could express them mathematically, on the model of Newton's physics, as the obvious path to a truly scientific medicine. The heart, which drives the blood, is clearly the motor of the body, which he thought of, using a hydraulic image, in terms of 'canals and fluids'.[33] To Pitcairne life was equivalent to circulation; he was convinced, for example, that animal heat arises from the friction of the blood with the walls of its vessels and is therefore a function of its velocity. The conception of secretion, whereby other fluids, which also circulate, derive from the blood, was central to his mechanistic physiology. Secretion, he asserted, occurs 'merely by the Force which the Heart impresses upon the Blood, which compels all Fluids to endeavour to pass thro' those Parts where there is the least Power of Resistance.'[34]

Nehemiah Grew, one of the pioneering microscopists, was convinced that he saw a network of tiny vessels when he looked at woody substances through his instrument, and he employed a similar set of concepts to develop a system of vegetable physiology. As he portrayed plant life, sap is elaborated in the root by a process of fermentation produced by a mechanical circulation. When it is mature, the sap is forced up through the fibres of the trunk and out through the branches until it becomes the matter of leaves. It is obvious that Grew had the circulation of the blood much in mind, and like Harvey he used the metaphor of machinery to discuss vegetable life.

> But were there no Leaves to make a free reception of the Sap, it must needs be stagnant in all the Parts to the Root, and so the Root being clogg'd, its fermenting and other Offices will be voyded, and so the due Growth of the whole. As in the motion of a Watch, although the original term thereof be the Spring, yet the capacity for the continuance in a due measure throughout all the Wheels, is the free and easie motion of the Ballance.[35]

The whole tenor of the age led Grew to see the structure of wood as a set of pipes through which fluids must flow. 'For to what end are Vessels,' he asked, 'but for the conveyance of Liquor?'[36]

For the ultimate expression of the mechanical preconceptions of the age, however, look back to the physical sciences and to one of the leaders of the scientific revolution, Christiaan Huygens. The son of Descartes's patron, Constantijn Huygens, Christiaan met the French philosopher in his own home when he was still a boy, and he enlisted in the new programme without reserve. Toward the end of his life, Huygens recalled how he had gradually become disillusioned with Descartes, as he discovered more and more things in his philosophy that were false, 'and now I find almost nothing in all his physics that I can accept as true, nor in his metaphysics and his meteorology.'[37] The process of disillusionment was already well advanced in 1669 when Huygens followed two other scientists in presenting a discussion of the nature of gravity before the *Académie* in Paris. Roberval and Frénicle before him both argued that the heaviness of bodies, whereby they descend toward the earth, is caused by an attraction between them and the earth. Huygens may have come to reject Descartes, but the opening lines of his own discourse on gravity, though they were too long to be a battle cry, did express, in their scorn for any concept of attraction, the basic passion that animated the mechanical philosophy.

> To discover a cause of weight that is intelligible, it is necessary to investigate how weight can come about, while assuming the existence only of bodies made of one common matter in which one admits no quality or inclination to approach each other but solely different sizes, figures, and motions . . .[38]

Or better yet consider the cryptic note he set down twenty years later as he read another theory of attractions, Newton's *Principia*. To scientists of Huygens's generation the theory of vortices appeared as the very foundation of any mechanical philosophy. Book II of the *Principia* demonstrated from first principles of dynamics that a material vortex was, on the one hand, incapable of sustaining itself and, on the other, incompatible with the observed phenomena of the solar system, and Huygens was much too good a scientist not to recognize the force of the demonstration. We can take his note as a measure of the permanent impact of Descartes's new vision of nature even on those who realized Descartes's own shortcomings: 'Vortices destroyed by Newton. Vortices of spherical motion in their place'.[39]

Let me add that Newton had felt the impact of the new vision as much as Huygens, and if he rejected vortices, admitted the existence of forces of attraction and repulsion, and made other modifications, he too continued to think of a universe that consisted of particles of one common matter in motion, the central proposition of the mechanical philosophy.

In addition to quantifying and mechanizing nature, the seventeenth century also accepted nature as other, that is as alien in virtually every respect to the reality the species that studies nature thought it experienced. Consider our Scholastic philosopher once more. The world he discussed, like the world Aristotle had analysed two thousand years earlier, was the world of daily experience and common sense. It was of course geocentric. It was qualitative rather than quantitative; the Scholastic assumed, for an observer that is both sound and competent, a one-to-one correspondence between appearance and reality. Although he did not explicitly state as much in the manuscript, our Scholastic undoubtedly accepted one important feature that had not been in Aristotle, that the whole universe had been created as the stage on which mankind would play out the great drama of salvation. Rather than diminishing the proportion between mankind and nature, the Christian element in the conception increased the sense of a universe scaled to humanity.

Early in the seventeenth century Descartes made it his primary business in natural philosophy to challenge the affinity of the natural order to the human observer. This was the issue on which he chose to open his first exposition of his natural philosophy, *The world*. This was the conclusion to which both the *Meditations* and the *Principles of philosophy* built. In one sense it is merely another dimension of the mechanization of nature. As Descartes concluded in the Sixth Meditation, it is necessary that a world external to ourselves exists, but there is no necessity that it be in any way similar to the world our senses depict.[40] We seem to live in a world filled with life and with qualities. They are only appearances. Particles of matter can join together in complex structures that perform by mechanical necessity all of the phenomena we associate with life. Similar particles can impinge on the nerve endings of sentient beings to cause sensations to which we have attached the names of qualities, projecting human experience onto the world and mistaking it for reality. All of these things are rather mere appearances. Reality consists solely of inert particles of matter in motion. It could hardly be more different from the common sense world of daily experience in which our Scholastic philosopher thought he lived.

In fact, it could be far more different. Late in the century Newton shook off the authority of Descartes in natural philosophy, but far from returning him to the earlier view of nature, the rejection of Descartes led Newton into a world still more alien. For example, he began to reason seriously about the relative specific gravities of bodies. Gold, the densest body he knew, cannot be completely solid since thin sheets of gold are translucent. Assume for a moment that gold is half solid and half void. Gold is nineteen times as dense as water; water then can have at most one part of solid matter in thirty eight. As Newton liked to remark here, water cannot be compressed. In fact he was convinced that water cannot come close to one solid part in thirty eight, for water transmits light in straight lines at every angle. Newton ended up with a picture of bodies as extremely fine three-dimensional nets composed of infinitesimally small particles held together by forces of attraction. The continuation of planetary motions unaltered over millenia convinced him further that most of the universe does not contain even these diaphanous veils. It is rather an infinite void seasoned here and there with the barest suggestions of solid matter. Early in the eighteenth century, a popularizer of the Newtonian natural philosophy argued that if all of the solid matter in the universe were compacted together it would not fill a nut shell.[41]

Mere size is another measure of otherness. A medieval writer had indicated the size of the universe by imagining that Adam set out from the centre on the day of creation, which he placed in 5199 BC, walking along a radius at a rate of twenty-five miles a day.[42] By the middle of the thirteenth century he would have covered nearly sixty million miles but would still have more than 700 years or six and a half million miles left to the perimeter. To the medieval mind, of course, the calculation revealed the immensity of the universe—not an unimaginable immensity, however, rather an all too imaginable one, an immensity proportioned, like the rest of the medieval universe, to the human scale.

In contrast, at the end of the seventeenth century, Francis Roberts calculated what the least distance of the nearest star could be from the absense of parallax even when powerful telescopes were used. Roberts's result was anything but extreme for the late seventeenth century; a few years earlier Christian Huygens placed the nearest star more than four times as far away. Roberts stated his result in units similar to those we still employ, the distance light will travel in a set period of time. He had a good idea of what the velocity of light is. In 1676 the Danish astronomer, Ole Roemer, had noticed that the observed period of Jupiter's first satellite, the one on which he concentrated, increases when Jupiter is receding from the earth and decreases when Jupiter is approaching. He interpreted the phenomenon as a consequence of the finite velocity of light and from it he computed the time it takes light to travel from the sun to the earth, which was equivalent to a velocity of 48 203 leagues per second, or (in later units) about 214 000 kilometres per second.[43] I might point to the calculation in passing as another instance of the quantification of nature. Partly because the accepted distance of the earth from the sun was too small and partly because of the difficulties the satellites involved, Roemer's figure was low, about seventy-one per cent of the velocity we now accept, but it had the right order of magnitude. According to it, light takes a little over seven minutes to travel the distance Adam would have walked since the day of creation, or a bit over sixteen minutes to travel entirely across the medieval universe from one side to the other. Against that background understand the import of Roberts's calculation, that light, not from the edge of the universe, for he did not believe it had an edge, but from the nearest star, takes longer to reach us than it took a ship, at the end of the seventeenth century, to sail to the West Indies, that is, more than six weeks.[44]

The scientific revolution vaulted beyond the scale of human experience in other directions as well. One of Leeuwenhoek's letters offers as good an example of the alien character of the new conception of nature as we are likely to find. Writing to the Royal Society, Leeuwenhoek mentioned that he had sometimes shown the little eels in vinegar to women, some of whom were so disgusted that they vowed never to use vinegar again. 'But what if in future,' he wondered, 'one should tell such people that there are living more animals in the unclean matter on the teeth in one's mouth, than there are men in a whole Kingdom?'[45]

I have attempted to note in passing lines of affinity between the separate features of the new conception of nature. Certainly I regard them not as isolated phenomena but rather as separate expressions of an integrated whole. The final feature, which I cannot imagine how to omit and still be true to the seventeenth century, the secularization of nature, appears somewhat different in this respect. The tensions between modern science and Christianity parallel those between Aristotelian natural philosophy and Christianity during earlier centuries. Given the social, ecclesiastical, and spiritual realities of the Middle Ages, the secularizing tendencies of Aristotelian philosophy—perhaps they are present in every sophisticated natural philosophy—had inevitably been contained. If that was not the case in the seventeenth century, the new realities of the age probably had more to do with the outcome than the new conception of nature.

Clearly one must speak with some care on the topic of secularization. Everyone is familiar with the religious proclivities of scientists, especially English scientists, in the late seventeenth century. The period has been called the golden age of natural theology, and with good cause. Never has atheism been so roundly refuted. One scientist after another took up his pen to demonstrate the existence of God, and what matters to me here, they called upon the latest findings of science to frame their arguments. Robert Boyle, the greatest chemist of his age and a most prolific author, inserted demonstrations of the existence of God, drawn not so much from chemistry as from natural philosophy in general, into nearly every one of his numerous books.[46] John Ray, the leading naturalist of the second half of the century, poured his extensive knowledge of the organic world into *The wisdom of God manifested in the works of the creation* (1691). William Derham and Bernard Nieuwentijdt were not scientists of the same order as Boyle and Ray, but they based their natural theology on competent expositions of the whole range of contemporary science.[47] Isaac Newton chose to add a General Scholium to the second edition of his *Principia* as a sort of conclusion to the work. It cannot be conceived, he asserted as he looked out over the universe whose laws he had demonstrated, 'that mere mechanical causes could give birth to so many regular motions . . . This most beautiful system of the sun, planets, and comets, could only proceed from the counsel and dominion of an intelligent and powerful Being.'[48]

All of this is undoubtedly true, and I have no magic wand that can conjure it away. I contend nevertheless that the meaning of it all is the secularization of nature, by which I mean to say that the scientific revolution effectively severed the cord that had bound the study of nature in Europe to Christianity during the previous millenium. The natural theology appears to me as a manifestation of the secularization rather than its denial, the effort of men uneasily aware that the ground was shifting under the traditional foundations of Christianity to construct new ones.

There are various levels on which one could pursue this theme. The conception of God is one of them. At the culmination of the scientific revolution, Isaac Newton was convinced that God must be actively present in every phenomenon of nature. It was inconceivable to him that a body composed of inert matter could act upon another at a distance to attract or repel it without some medium between them to transmit the action. He was equally convinced that he had disproved the possibility that the medium could be material. As it appears to me then, Newton conceived of God as the immediate cause of the forces of attraction and repulsion that he made the primary agents in nature.

A passage in the Thirty-first Query, in which Newton spoke of the need for periodic reformations of nature to correct irregularities that appear from the operation of natural laws, is well known.[49] It seems to me that its significance has been greatly exaggerated, to the extent that its meaning has been distorted. Newton was quite explicit that such reformations were extremely rare. They were necessary, he insisted, only after many ages, and he did not point to any instance in which one had yet occurred. The primary and overwhelming function of God, in Newton's view, was the maintenance of the regular operation of nature, what he called in the same passage its 'wonderful Uniformity', not intervention to alter the regular order. The active presence of God and the maintenance of the regular order were, with the exception of the hypothetical interventions, which had in fact never occurred, one and the same thing.

Newton's conception of God was not simple. The descriptive word that he used in the General Scholium was Pantocrator, the autocrat of the universe, whose arbitrary will is not bound by the precepts of human rationality—a conception of God with manifest overtones of the Old Testament's Yahweh. There were, however, fewer overtones from the New Testament. Surely it is significant that Newton rejected the doctrine of the Trinity. When we compare his Pantocrator with the redeeming God of Christian tradition, Newton's deity is beginning to look, to me at least, rather like an abstract metaphysical principle which justifies the regular operation of nature, a principle about which nothing distinct from the regular order can be asserted.[50] If later philosophers, heirs of the seventeenth century's difficult and painful struggle with theology, heirs for whom the concept of Pantocrator no longer bore any meaning—and such men were active already by the time of Newton's death—denied the necessity of the metaphysical principle, they did not have to alter anything at all in the picture of nature.

Let me, however, approach the issue on a different plane, the locus of authority in science. To be sure, this issue does not deal immediately with the conception of nature, but it has everything to do with Christianity and science and through this reflects directly on a secularized nature. I turn to our ideal Scholastic philosopher one last time. You will not be surprised to learn that, though he implicitly recognized the function of observation by setting as his goal a natural philosophy that squares with nature, on every question raised he cited the opinion of Aristotle, which he usually concluded by upholding. Usually, but not always, for he also recognized another authority higher than Aristotle, to wit, Christianity. Though our philosopher would not have hesitated for a moment to agree with Galileo (in a later mode) that nature, as the creation of God, is also His revelation, he did not even consider using nature as an authority independent of Scripture and the Church. Thus, to cite one example where at least a hundred are available, our philosopher refused to accept the proposition that the world is eternal and perfect. Rather, as Christianity teaches, it was created in time by an almighty God whose omnipotence is such that he could have created an infinity of other worlds more perfect.[51]

About twenty-five years after he compiled the manuscript commentary, Galileo faced the same issue from the other side. In 1615, he was denounced to the Inquisition, and out of the investigation of Galileo by the Holy Office came the Church's condemnation of Copernicanism. The moving force behind the Church's action was Cardinal Roberto Bellarmino, a man both of immense learning and of powerful intellect. On this issue, Bellarmino offers a more concrete representative of the earlier outlook than the faceless Scholastic of Galileo's manuscript.

As the case against Galileo heated up early in 1615, a Carmelite theologian, Paolo Foscarini, wrote a pamphlet on Copernican astronomy and Scripture in defense of the Florentine scientist and sent a copy to Bellarmino for comment. Bellarmino's letter to Foscarini, addressed to Galileo as much as to the theologian, reminded both men that the Council of Trent had forbidden the interpretation of Scripture in a way contrary to the common opinion of the Fathers, but that all of the Fathers agreed in interpreting the passages critical for Copernicanism as saying that the sun revolves around the earth, which is at rest. It would not do, he continued, to say that this is not a matter of faith. He who denies that Abraham had two sons and Jacob twelve is as much a heretic as he who denies the virgin birth of Christ, 'because it is the Holy Spirit who makes known both truths by the mouth of the Prophets and Apostles.'[52]

A year after the Church's condemnation of Copernicanism, Bellarmino had occasion in a different context to comment on the size of the moon. He knew that astronomers considered it to be, next to Mercury, the smallest body in the heavens, but he also knew that Scripture referred to the moon and the sun as the two 'luminaria magna'. Therefore he had no doubt that it ranked with the sun in size and exceeded every other planet. Do not object to me that astronomers disagree, he declared. They cannot demonstrate their opinion. 'Besides did not St. Augustine (*De Genesi ad litteram* , XXI, 16) say that is is much better to believe the Scriptures than the astrologers with respect to the size of the Moon.'[53]

Bellarmino was not saying anything from which the overwhelming majority, Catholic or Protestant, would have dissented at the beginning of the seventeenth century; he was sure enough of his position to lead the Church to condemn Copernicanism because it was inconsistent with the overt meaning of certain passages in Scripture.

One year short of a century after Bellarmino composed his letter to Foscarini, an Englishman, William Derham, who was also a cleric, published *Astro-theology: or a demonstration of the being and attributes of God, from a survey of the heavens*. You may be sure that Derham, as his title promised, surveyed the heavens rather than the Scriptures to prepare his argument. He even supplied himself with Huygens's 126 foot lens for that purpose, though in fact he spent more time surveying the latest literature on astronomy. In the Preface he cited those passages in the Bible which had troubled Bellarmino a hundred years before, but Derham cited them only to dismiss them. It is not the purpose of Scripture to teach philosophy, and when it speaks of the heavens it adopts the common people's language of appearances.[54] The passage in Scripture that seemed relevant to Derham was the opening line of Psalm 19:'The heavens declare the glory of God.'[55] He considered not just the Copernican system, but the Copernican system set in a myriad of other heliocentric systems that stretched out in every direction with no limit, the one most conducive to the glory of God.[56] As he pursued the theme, Derham found occasion to cite Cicero and Seneca, with their appeal to the observed order of the heavens, at least twice as much as he cited the Bible, and the few passages he did cite from Scripture were used as illustrations of the argument rather than determinants. I might note that Derham, an Anglican clergyman, did his best to Christianize an argument not inherently Christian.[57] Nevertheless, the god whose being and attributes he found in the immensity and order of the heavens did not have much in common with Bellarmino's redeeming God who became flesh and dwelt among us.

Rather than Derham, however, take as the image of the new conception the correspondence between the Rev. Thomas Burnet, author of *Telluris theoria sacra*, and Isaac Newton in December 1680 and January 1681. Burnet had done more than convince himself that he should look to nature rather than the Bible to understand how the present earth came into being; he had convinced himself as well that the story of the creation in *Genesis* was a fable, composed by Moses for political purposes, which did not relate the true order of events. Newton, on the contrary, attempted to justify the Mosaic account to Burnet. He agreed without further ado that Moses had cast his story in the idiom of the common people, but he argued that Moses' story, despite the idiom, was consistent with what science, primarily chemistry in this case, the field of science that had dominated Newton's attention during the previous decade, would lead us to expect.[58] Compare the assumptions of both Burnet and Newton with those of Bellarmino less than seventy years earlier. They had exactly reversed the roles of Scripture and science. Instead of using Scripture to decide what is true in science, they used science, knowledge they had drawn from the consideration of nature, to judge what was true in Scripture. That is what I have in mind when I speak of the secularization of nature.

More than any other one man, Isaac Newton drew the various strands of the scientific revolution's conception of nature together, roughly a century after Galileo compiled the manuscript I have cited, and wove them into a cohesive fabric, the modern scientific picture of nature. Although it has been modified greatly in its details in the intervening three centuries, it is still with us, the very foundation of intellectual life in the West and increasingly in the whole world. Early in the eighteenth century, a series of popularizers attempted to educate the public in the new world view.[59] Their books make interesting reading. How similar they sound to the twentieth-century authors who have undertaken to interpret another strange new world to the non-scientific public. That is, the Newtonian world, which we have learned over the space of three hundred years to regard as the essence of common sense, appeared just as foreign to its age as four-dimensional space–time continua and quantum mechanics, not to mention later exotica such as quarks, superstrings, and all the rest, appear to those of us today without advanced degrees in physics. A world conceived as the arena in which Christians pursue the ultimate goal of eternal salvation had been quantified, mechanized, perceived to be other, secularized, that is, altered beyond recognition, all in the short space of a hundred years. I am not aware that all of history can offer another example of a transformation of human thought so radical, or of one fraught with equal significance.

NOTES

1. I. Bernard Cohen, *Revolution in science* (Harvard University Press, Cambridge, MA 1988). See especially Chapter 5, 'The scientific revolution: the first recognition of revolution in science.'
2. See, for example, Robert K. Merton, *Science, technology, and society in seventeenth century England*, (Harper and Row, New York, 1970), published originally in *Osiris*, **4** (1938); and Charles Webster, *The great instauration* (Duckworth, London, 1975). There are innumerable other studies concerned with the Puritan thesis and allied themes.
3. Boris Hessen [Gessen], *The social and economic roots of Newton's Principia* (Fertig, New York 1971), published originally in the volume, *Science at the crossroads* (Kniga, London 1931), is a famous Marxian statement of this thesis. If the Marxian insistence on the controlling importance of material or economic factors in history has been the principal source of this interpretation, the influence of the insight, in the history of science as in virtually every branch of history, has spread far beyond Marxian circles. For other studies that emphasize the social context of the scientific revolution, which are far too numerous to list here exhaustively, see Leonardo Olschki, *Geschichte der neusprachlichen wissenschaftlichen Literatur*, 3 volumes (C. Winter, Heidelberg and Leipzig, 1919–27); a number of articles by Edgar Zilsel including 'The sociological roots of science', *American Journal of Sociology*, **47** (1941–2), 544–62; J. D. Bernal, *Science in history* (London 1951), Part IV, 'The birth of modern science'; and more recently two books by Margaret Jacob, *The Newtonians and the English revolution* (Cornell University Press, Ithaca, NY 1976), and *The cultural meaning of the scientific revolution* (Knopf, New York 1987).
4. The interpretations are not mutually exclusive. Both Merton and Webster, cited above, lay great stress on the practical applications of science during the seventeenth century. See also, for a somewhat different argument linking science and technology, Paolo Rossi,

Philosophy, technology, and the arts in the early modern era, trans. Salvator Attanasio (Harper and Row, New York 1970).

5. On the day after I wrote these lines, I happened, for other purposes, to be reading Francisco Guerra, *Nicolas Bautista Monardes. Su vida y su obra* (Compañia Fundidora de Fierro y Aciero de Monterrey, Mexico City 1961). In a passage (p. 91) that begins with a discussion of the sixteenth century Spanish physicians, Francisco Hernandez and José Acosta, the seventeenth century Dutch physician, Willem Piso, and the German, Georg Markgraf, who was associated with Piso in Brazil, Guerra goes on to name twenty-one other Spaniards, many of whom I suspect were physicians, who contributed to European knowledge of the natural history of the western hemisphere. With the exception of Hernandez and Acosta, I have never heard of any of the Spaniards, and I believe that other Anglo-Saxon historians of science know them just as little as I do. It did not take a Puritan ethic to set them to work; apparently the botanical-pharmacological tradition, which was especially strong within medicine but not confined to it, was quite sufficient. Three weeks after writing the note above, I returned to it soon after reading about the career of Ulisse Aldrovandi. (L. Frati, 'La vita di U. Aldrovandi' in *Intorno alla vita e alle opere di Ulisse Aldrovandi* (L. Beltrami, Bologna 1907), and also other articles in this volume.) He needed the Puritan ethic just as little as the Spanish physicians.
6. E. A. Burtt, *The metaphysical foundations of modern physical science* (K. Paul, Trench, Trubner, London 1924). Alexandre Koyré, *Études Galiléennes* (Hermann, Paris 1939). In fact, Koyré's phase in the *Études* was 'geometrization of space'. The broader concept seems to me to be implicit throughout this book and later ones that he wrote, however.
7. Johannes Kepler, *Harmonice mundi*, Bk. IV, Chapter 1; *Gesammelte Werke*, ed. Max Caspar, 19 volumes (C. H. Beck, Munich 1937–83), Vol. 6, p. 233.
8. *The assayer; Discoveries and opinions of Galileo*, trans. and ed. Stillman Drake (Doubleday, Garden City, NY 1957), pp. 237–8.
9. *Le opere de Galileo Galilei*, ed. Antonio Favaro, 20 volumes (Barbèra, Florence 1890–1909), vol. 1, pp. 15–177. The reader will understand that this was a private manuscript that Galileo compiled for his own use and never attempted to put out as his own work. It has been published only in our age.
10. William A. Wallace, *Galileo's early notebooks: the physical questions*, (University of Notre Dame Press, Notre Dame, IN 1977). Adriano Carugo and Alistair Crombie, 'The Jesuits and Galileo's ideas of

science and of nature', *Annali dell'Istituto e Museo di Storia della Scienza di Firenze*, **8.2** (1983) 3–68.

11. Wallace, *Notebooks*, pp. 220–1 and 247 (see note 10).
12. Leeuwenhoek to Henry Oldenburg, 9 October 1676; *The collected letters of Antoni van Leeuwenhoek*, 11 volumes continuing (Swets and Zeitlinger, Amsterdam 1939–), vol. 2, p. 73. Following the Dutch original, I have added 'more than' to the English translation here.
13. Ibid., p. 101.
14. Ibid., p. 115.
15. Leeuwenhoek to Constantijn Huygens, 26 December 1678; ibid., p. 403.
16. Leeuwenhoek to Henry Oldenburg, 23 March 1677; ibid., pp. 199–201.
17. Leeuwenhoek to Robert Hooke, 12 November 1680; ibid., vol. 3, pp. 335–7. A. Schierbeek was impressed enough by the quantitative aspect of Leeuwenhoek to name his study *Measuring the invisible world* (Abeland-Schuman, New York 1959).
18. Hooke, *Micrographia* (J. Martyn and J. Allestry, London 1665), pp. 49–54.
19. I cite from my own article, 'Isaac Newton's coloured circles twixt two contiguous glasses', *Archive for History of Exact Sciences*, **2** (1965) 181–96, most of which is the publication of Newton's record of his first sustained experiments with the rings.
20. The first ring varied somewhat more; it was always a problem in these experiments, since he had to press down hard to bring the lens into contact with the sheet of glass, distorting the two where they touched. Newton also succeeded in tracing the source of this apparent inconsistency in his measurements.
21. Galileo, *Dialogue concerning the two chief world systems*, trans. Stillman Drake, 2nd edn. (University of California Press, Berkeley, CA 1967), pp. 190–203. Newton found it in Salusbury's translation (Thomas Salusbury, *Mathematical collections and translations* (W. Leybourne, London 1661), vol. 1, pp. 167–80). Neither Newton nor those before him used the phrase 'centrifugal force', which Christian Huygens coined. I use it here for convenience; they spoke of the tendency of bodies in circular motion to recede from the centre. Like Huygens, Newton still thought of circular motion in terms of centrifugal rather than centripetal force at the time he composed the manuscript in question here. The quantitative measure of centrifugal force, as Huygens and Newton demonstrated, was identical with the formula we still use for centripetal force.

22. John Herivel, *Background to Newton's 'Principia,'* (Oxford University Press, Oxford 1965, pp. 129–32.
23. Cambridge University Library, *Add. MS. 3958*, f. 45. The manuscript is published with a photographic reproduction in *The correspondence of Isaac Newton*, ed. H. W. Turnbull, *et al.,* 7 volumes (Cambridge University Press, 1959–77), vol. 3, pp. 46–54. It is also published in Herivel, *Background*, pp. 183–91 (see note 22).
24. Newton measured the periods of two pendulums of different length, both of which, obviously, could not complete 1512 swings in exactly one hour. Newton used the number 1512 for both, and calculated in each case how much the time for that number of swings differed from one hour.
25. Richard S. Westfall, 'Newton and the acceleration of gravity', *Archive for the History of Exact Sciences*, **35** 1986) 255–72.
26. Descartes, *Discourse on method*; *The philosophical works of Descartes*, trans. Elizabeth S. Haldane and G. R. T. Ross (Dover, New York 1955), vol. 1, p. 90.
27. The majority of Boyle's many works are partly or wholly devoted to these themes, but see especially *The origin of forms and qualities* (1666) (*The works of the honourable Robert Boyle*, 5 volumes (London 1744), vol. 2, pp. 451–542), *Of the excellency and grounds of the corpuscular or mechanical philosophy* (1674) (ibid., vol. 3, pp. 449–57), *Experiments, notes, &c. about the mechanical origin or production of divers particular qualities* (1675) (ibid., vol. 3, pp. 565–632), and any or all of his various histories of specific qualities such as colours.
28. Wallace, *Notebook*, pp. 209–10, 216–17 (see note 10).
29. Descartes, *Treatise on Man*, trans. Thomas Steele Hall, (Harvard University Press, Cambridge, MA 1972), p. 113.
30. Mayow, *Medico-physical works*, re-issue ed. (Alembic Club, Edinburgh and London 1957); see especially the first Treatise, 'On sal nitrum and nitro-aerial spirit', and also the Fourth Treatise, 'On muscular motion and animal spirits'.
31. Borelli, *De motu animalium*, 2 volumes (Bernabò, Rome 1680–1), Vol. 1, pp. 277–80.
32. Bellini, *De urinis et pulsibus, de missione sanquinis*, ... (Pisarri, Bologna 1683) and *A mechanical account of fevers*, trans. (Bell, Senex, Taylor and Ostorn, London 1720). The discussion of Bellini and of Pitcairne which follows relies primarily on the doctoral dissertation, *Newtonian matter theory, chemistry and medicine, 1690–1713*, of my student Anita Guerrini (Indiana University).
33. *Medicinae elementorum physico-mathematicorum brevis conspectio*;

Archibaldi Pitcarnii opera omnia medica, (J. A. Langerak, Leiden 1737), p. 6.

34. *Dissertatio de motu, quo cibi in ventriculo rediguntur ad formam sanguini reficiendo idoneam*, ibid., p. 245. English from *Works*, trans. George Sewell and J. T. Desaguliers (E. Curll, London 1715), p. 103. See Anita Guerrini, 'Archibald Pitcairne and Newtonian Medicine', *Medical History*, **31** (1987) 70–83.
35. Grew, *The anatomy of plants* (W. Rawlins, London 1682), p. 33.
36. Ibid., p. 25.
37. A set of comments written in 1693 on Baillet's biography of Descartes; Huygens, *Oeuvres complètes*, 22 volumes (Nyhoff, La Haye, 1888–1950), Vol. 10, p. 403.
38. Ibid., vol. 19, p. 631.
39. Ibid., vol. 21, p. 437.
40. *Philosophical Works*, vol. 1, p. 191 (see note 26).
41. I have allowed myself here to use a striking phrase that was not coined in the early eighteenth century but rather by Joseph Priestley (*Disquisitions relating to matter and spirit*, (J. Johnson, London 1777, p. 17). The identical concept without that figure appeared in Henry Pemberton, *A view of Sir Isaac Newton's philosophy* (S. Palmer, London 1728), pp. 355–6. Before Pemberton, John Keill had suggested how little solid matter there may be in the world (*An introduction to natural philosophy* (Innys, London 1720), pp. 63–7; the original Latin version of Keill's work, *Introductio ad veram physicam*, appeared in 1702), and Francesco Algarotti advanced much the same concept in *Il newtonianismo per le dame* (G. Pasquale, Naples 1737), (*The philosophy of Sir Isaac Newton explained*, trans. Elizabeth Carter (R. Urie, Glasgow 1765), pp. 235–6).
42. Gossouin of Metz, *Image du monde*; I cite from Albert van Helden, *Measuring the universe: cosmic dimensions from Aristarchus to Halley* (University of Chicago Press, Chicago, IL 1985), pp. 37–8.
43. 'Demonstration touchant le mouvement de la lumière trouvé par M. Romer de l'Académie Royale des Sciences', *Journal des scavans*, 7 December 1676, pp. 233–6. See I. Bernard Cohen, *Roemer and the first determination of the velocity of light* (Burndy Library, New York 1944); the pamphlet includes a reproduction of the announcement in the *Journal des scavans*.
44. Francis Roberts, 'Concerning the distance of the fixed stars', *Philosophical Transactions*, **18** (1694) 101–3.
45. Leeuwenhoek to Francis Aston, 17 September 1683; *Collected Letters*, Vol. 4, p. 135 (see note 12).

46. There is no point in attempting to list every relevant book by Boyle. See especially *The Christian virtuoso* (1690) (*Works*, vol. 5, pp. 37–74, see note 27) which sums them all up near the end of his life. On this aspect of Boyle, who has received more scholarly attention in relation to natural theology than any other scientist of the late seventeenth century, see in addition to the many discussions that appear in works not devoted exclusively to this issue or to Boyle, Mitchell S. Fisher, *Robert Boyle, devout naturalist*, (Oshiver Studio Press, Philadelphia, PA 1945); Harold Fisch, 'The scientist as priest: a note on Robert Boyle', *Isis*, **44** (1953) 252–65; Richard McMasters Hunt, *The place of religion in the science of Robert Boyle*, (University of Pittsburgh Press, Pittsburgh, PA 1955); Mary Elizabeth Bowen, *This great automaton, the world: the mechanical philosophy of Robert Boyle, F.R.S.*, Columbia University Ph.D., 1976; and the pertinent sections of my own book, *Science and religion in seventeenth century England*, (Yale University Press, New Haven, 1958). On the general theme see Amos Funkenstein, *Theology and the scientific imagination from the Middle Ages to the seventeenth century* (Princeton University Press, Princeton, NJ 1986). Keith Hutchison offers an interpretation at odds with mine, 'Supernaturalism and the mechanical philosophy', *History of Science*, **21** (1983) 297–333.
47. Derham, *Physico-theology, or a demonstration of the being and attributes of God, from his works of creation* (W. Innys, London 1713). Nieuwentijdt, *Het regt gebruick der werelt beschouwing* (Wolters and Pauli, Amsterdam 1715), translated by John Chamberlayne as *The religious philosopher: or, the right use of contemplating the works of the Creator*, 3 volumes (J. Senex, London 1717).
48. Newton, *Mathematical principles of natural philosophy*, trans. Andrew Motte, revised Florian Cajori (University of California Press, Berkeley, CA 1934), p. 544.
49. *Opticks*, based on 4th edn. (Dover, New York 1952), p. 402.
50. In a different context Newton believed in the providential role of God in human history. This was the theme of his interpretation of the prophecies. See the discussion of his interpretation in my biography of Newton, *Never at rest* (Cambridge University Press, Cambridge, 1980), Chapter 8. I am unable to see that Newton brought the providential God of human history into harmony with the God of nature. Thus he was ready to turn to Scripture (that is, the prophecies) for the interpretation of history; I am not aware that he ever looked in Scripture for the understanding of nature.
51. Wallace, *Notebook*, pp. 43–8 (see note 10). The position of our

Scholastic here does not differ all that much from Newton's. During the Middle Ages and through the sixteenth century, the authority of Christianity kept the naturalism of Aristotelian philosophy in check. With Newton the new natural philosophy still accepted part of that authority; one of the animating passions of his life was resistance to the naturalism in Descartes's philosophy. I am arguing that Newton nevertheless went a considerable distance toward identifying God with the natural order so that the difference from naturalism consisted mostly of the mere assertion of spiritual dominion. Denial of the assertion altered nothing in the natural philosophy. During the eighteenth century the authority of Christianity was thrown almost entirely aside as far as science was concerned.

52. Bellarmino to Foscarini, 12 April 1615; *Le opere di Galileo Galilei*, vol. 12, pp. 171–2 (see role 9). The letter is translated in full in James Brodrick, *Robert Bellarmine, saint and scholar* (Newman Press, Westminster, MD 1961), pp. 360–3.
53. Quoted in Ugo Baldini and George V. Coyne, 'The Louvain lectures (Lectiones Lovanienses) of Bellarmine and the autograph copy of his 1616 Declaration to Galileo', *Vatican Observatory Publications: Studi Galileiani*, **1** (1984) 45. Forty-five years earlier, when he lectured at Louvain, Bellarmino had discussed the same issue and arrived at the same conclusion; ibid., p. 22.
54. I did not have access to the first edition. Derham, *Astro-theology* (W. Innys, London 1715), pp. xxi–xxxiv.
55. Ibid., p. 1. Near the end of the book (p. 203) Derham rounded out his argument by returning to this passage.
56. Ibid., pp. xliv–xlv.
57. See especially the final chapter (pp. 227–8) which, apropos of nothing else in the book, concludes that we should aspire after the heavenly state.
58. Newton to Burnet, 24 December 1680; Burnet to Newton, 13 January 1681; Newton to Burnet, January 1681; *The correspondence of Isaac Newton*, vol. 2, pp. 319, 321–8, 329–35.
59. John Keill (1702), Pemberton (1728), and Algarotti (1737), see note 41 above; Voltaire, *Elémens de la philosophie de Neuton* (J. Desbordes, Amsterdam 1738) (*The elements of Sir Isaac Newton's philosophy* (S. Austin, London 1738)); Colin Maclaurin, *An account of Sir Isaac Newton's philosophy* (Maclaurin's children, London 1748).

4

Darwin's Nature

ELLIOTT R. SOBER
Philosophy Department, University of Wisconsin, Madison

It is a simplification, though a useful one, to see etymologies as the fossil traces of extinct theories. This, perhaps, is part of what Quine meant in his epigram to *Word and object*—ontology recapitulates philosophy.

One use of the concept of *nature* is embodied in the idea that the entire world is populated by objects that have *natures*. There is the nature of matter, the nature of life, and also, there is human nature. This meaning of the term carries with it a vestige of essentialism. I will return to the issue of essentialism at the end; it is not where I wish to begin.

The concept of nature I want first to consider contrasts nature with *artifice*. An artifice (or artifact) is the work of an artific*er*. It is the product of intelligence—of skills. Flowers are part of nature; artificial flowers are human handiwork. Although this use of the pair of terms suggests that they are mutually exclusive, standard varieties of theism elide them. If God created the world, then nature is itself an artifact; it is the product of intelligent design.

The idea that God the artificer stands outside of the nature he created leaves open how human beings are related to the rest of the natural order. Even so, it was a persistent theme of the theological picture that Darwin learned from and ultimately reacted against that God created human beings and the rest of nature so that a particular relationship should prevail between them: *the rest of nature was a gift that God bestowed upon human beings*. Nature is to be understood in terms of the contribution it makes to human prosperity. Human beings are part of nature, but they occupy a unique position in the natural order.

This idea played a central role in English natural theology. In *The wisdom of God in the creation*, published in 1691, John Ray argued that plants and animals, as well as fire, wood, and metals were placed on earth because they would prove useful for human beings. One hundred and fifty years later, the Bridgewater author Charles Bell, in his *The hand: its mechanism and vital endowments, as evincing design*, developed the same idea—that human beings are the centre of the whole world system, which was arranged so as to harmonize with peculiarly human requirements. And in *Geology and mineralogy considered with reference to natural theology*, William Buckland argued in detail that the abundance and usefulness of coal could not be a coincidence, but showed that God long ago had laid in this treasure in anticipation of the needs that industrial civilization would come to manifest.[1]

What was Darwin's view of this picture—that God the artificer arranged nature for our benefit? True, there are occasional nods in Darwin's writings towards a God who stands behind the workings of evolution and natural selection. At the end of the *Origin of species* (pp. 488–9), he says 'to my mind it accords better with what we know of the laws impressed on matter by the Creator, that the production and extinction of the past and present inhabitants of the world should have been due to secondary causes, like those determining the birth and death of the individual. When I view all beings not as special creations, but as the lineal descendants of some few beings which lived long before the first bed of the Silurian system was deposited, they seem to me to become ennobled.' And when Darwin takes up the problem in *The descent of man* of how religious ideas were developed by primitive peoples, he is quick to insist (p. 65) that 'the question is of course wholly distinct from that higher one, whether there exists a Creator and Ruler of the universe; and this has been answered in the affirmative by the highest intellects that have ever lived.' In spite of these pronouncements, it would be a mistake to interpret these remarks as the expressions of a robust theism. Though Darwin was no village atheist, his religious convictions began to decline in young adulthood. Robert Richards's picture of the trajectory is an apt one: 'By the time he wrote the *Origin*, only a cautious Deism remained; and in the decade thereafter that too slid under, leaving but a wariness of the power of religion to promote or smite a scientific theory, a reverence for his wife's beliefs, and a polite agnosticism.'[2]

There is more to Darwin, or to any scientist, than the theories he propounded. Or to put the same point contrapositively, Darwin's theories are more austere in their content than the full range of beliefs that animated the man. Darwin's theological convictions are as they may be. But it is a separate question what his biological theories actually say about God the artificer and the relation of human beings to the rest of the living world. When we focus on the theories and not on the man, the problem shifts somewhat—from biography to the logic of a theoretical position.

What should we understand by the phrase 'Darwin's theories'? Certainly not everything that Darwin commented upon should be included, or else the just quoted passages from the *Origin* and *The descent of man* would show that Darwin had theories about the existence of God. Rather, I prefer to see Darwin as elaborating two fundamental hypotheses. The first is the hypothesis of *the tree of life*. It says that present day organisms are related. Take any two of them. If their ancestors are traced back far enough in time, a common ancestor will be found. Species are related to each other genealogically. The second hypothesis is the hypothesis of *natural selection*. If all life is related, the question arises of why living things are not identical in their morphology, physiology, and behaviour. Darwin's conjecture, roughly, was that populations live in different environments and that these environmental differences make a difference as to which variants arising in a population are favourable to survival and reproduction. Populations living in different environments diverge from each other, since the organisms in different populations adapt to different environments.

Darwin had much else to say about nature. Not only did he apply these two guiding ideas to numerous specific problems of natural history; in addition, he addressed himself to many other problems, such as the growth of coral reefs, that fall outside the scope of these two ideas.[3] None the less, I think it fair to say that these were the principal organizing ideas of Darwin's scientific work (an assessment which Darwin himself endorsed in his *Autobiography*). What are the theistic consequences of these two hypotheses?

Darwin's theories do not explicitly address the question of whether there is a God. His theories can be conjoined with theism without engendering a formal contradiction; so too can they be conjoined with atheism. From our vantage point a hundred years later, it is a familiar fact that scientific materialism often allied itself with atheism (think of Marx, Freud, and the logical positivists) and typically saw Darwin's theory as contributing to both. But it is important not to forget that many thinkers at least considered the possibility of embracing both Darwinism and theism. This idea was not always brushed aside as absurd and sophistical. On the contrary, many went the route of Darwin's American supporter, Asa Gray, who argued that Darwinism leads to atheism no more than Newtonianism does. When a billiards player sends a ball across the table, is the motion of the ball the result of design or of physical forces? Gray thought that the answer is *both*. Design is the ultimate cause; purely physical laws are proximal. By analogy, Gray and many others held that a beneficent deity had designed the laws of evolution.

So no logical contradiction is present in either conjunction—Darwinism *and* atheism or Darwinism *and* theism. But this does not mean that the two conjunctions are equally plausible. Darwinism does not force the acceptance of atheism, but does it incline in that direction?

To address this question, we must return Darwin's theories to the historical context in which they arose. Natural theology had relied fundamentally on the argument from design as its central demonstration of God's reality. William Paley's watch analogy is the best known representative of this line of thinking, which enjoyed a robust life for a hundred and fifty years or so. If you found a watch on a heath, you would not hesitate to conclude that it was the product of intelligent design. The exquisite arrangement of its parts, and the suitability of the whole to the task of telling time, cry out for explanation in terms of an intelligent watchmaker. By analogy, Paley argued in his *Natural theology*, organisms are complex machines that are well adapted to the task of surviving. They too demand explanation in terms of an intelligent designer, one far more skilled than the average watchmaker.

Hume earlier had criticized this line of argument in his *Dialogues concerning natural religion*, which were published posthumously in 1779. Although many philosophers now think that this masterpiece totally undercut the design argument, Hume's work was not generally perceived before Darwin as having this effect. One reason, perhaps, is that Hume offered no systematically worked out positive proposal for explaining apparent design. His work is largely negative in its goals. Whether the work succeeded in these negative objectives I will not discuss here.[4] But as a matter of history, the design argument not only survived the onslaught of Hume's corrosive scepticism; it prospered in the ensuing seventy-five years.

The logic of the design argument is, in the terminology of C. S. Peirce, *abductive*; it is an example of what philosophers now term inference to the best explanation. The existence of God is a hypothesis, whose plausibility rests on its ability to explain observations better than any other available explanation is able to do. The fact that God cannot be observed directly is quite irrelevant. Gregor Mendel never directly observed genes, but observing reproductive patterns in the pea plants in his garden provided ample evidence for the claim that genes exist.

Before Darwin, it could plausibly be maintained that the adaptedness of organisms to their environments required explanation in terms of intelligent design. No other competing hypothesis was available that could do the job. Darwin changed the dialectical landscape by introducing a thoroughly naturalistic and materialistic explanatory mechanism. It was no longer true that intelligent design was the only available explanation of adaptation.

Had natural theology placed only modest weight on the design argument, Darwin's theories would have had only slight or no implications about the tenability of theism. But the historical fact of the matter is that Darwin undercut the principal argument of natural theology. If theism earlier had been rendered plausible by the design argument, then Darwin's theories diminished the plausibility of theism.

The logic of this diminution is illustrated by a remark attributed to another scientist expounding another theory. The story is told of Laplace's describing to Napoleon how he, Laplace, had elaborated Newtonian ideas to solve various problems in celestial mechanics. Napoleon is said to have asked—'Where is God to be found in your theories?' Laplace replied that he had no need of such a hypothesis.

Ockham's Razor—the Principle of Parsimony—says that entities should not be postulated without necessity. The razor is a methodological maxim that helps flesh out what 'best' means in the phrase 'inference to the *best* explanation'. One explanation is better than another, all else being equal, when the first posits fewer entities and processes than the second.[5] Laplace wielded Ockham's razor in celestial mechanics just as Darwin did in connection with organismic adaptation. In both cases the excised entity was *God*.

To say that the postulate of God is eliminated from an explanation leaves open whether the appropriate conclusion is atheism or agnosticism. If there no longer is a need to postulate the existence of God, should we conclude that there is no God, or that we should suspend judgment on the question? Other scientists in other contexts have taken the razor to have negative implications about the existence of the excised entity. For example, in Einstein's 1905 paper on special relativity, he says that his theory shows the 'the introduction of a "luminiferous ether" will prove to be superfluous.'[6] This did not mean that scientists were supposed to suspend judgment on the ether; rather, the theory led to the conclusion that there is no such thing.

Were the design argument the only argument for the existence of God, Darwin's theory would lead directly to atheism. There is no need to follow Paley in his demand for an intelligent designer as an explanation of apparent design. The existence of God would be just as implausible as the existence of a luminiferous ether. But theism has always had its other arguments; and some theists hold that rational argument is an inappropriate tool to use in deciding whether God exists. Perhaps some other feature of the universe, besides the existence of adaptations, is plausibly explained by the theistic postulate. Darwin's theories do not address this question.

It is for this reason that the tree of life and the principle of natural selection, while undermining one prominent defence of theism, cannot be said to prove that theism is false.

There is another element in the theistic picture painted by natural theology that Darwin's theory more directly impugns. Not only did the tradition against which Darwin reacted describe nature as an artifact created by God; in addition, it held that the living world is as it is because of the good it does for human beings. Nature is a *gift* built by God for our benefit. This is the story told by Ray, Paley, Bell, Buckland, and others.

Darwin's theory contradicts this teleology, but not because Darwin totally excised teleological concepts from his science. If teleology played no role in his theories, then it might be possible to conjoin a teleological cosmogony with Darwin's science. The conflict arose precisely because of the way Darwin retained teleology and gave it a materialistic reading.

Darwin's theory entails that some objects exist in nature because of the benefits they confer. Human beings have opposable thumbs because thumbs did our ancestors some good. Darwin's concept of natural selection explains the presence of this trait by postulating an ancestral population in which some organisms have the trait while others do not. Ancestors with opposable thumbs were better able to survive and reproduce, so the trait gradually increased in frequency. Given long enough, the trait became universal in the population.

Darwin constantly posed and answered teleological questions. The theory of natural selection provides a materialistic framework for investigating questions of the form—'What is this thing *for*?' Where natural theologians had understood teleology as a manifestation of God's intentions, Darwinism sees teleology as arising as a product of natural selection.

The conflict between the teleology of natural theology and Darwin's teleology arose from the *kinds* of teleological hypotheses his theory would and would not tolerate. A part of an organism—such as an opposable thumb—could have a function. This part helped the whole of which it was a part—an organism—to survive and reproduce. But Darwin shied away from treating objects at higher levels of organization—organisms, or populations, or species—as evolving because of the benefits they conferred on objects at higher levels still.

That is to say, Darwin was fairly consistent in thinking of the organism as what would now be called *the unit of selection.*[7] Organisms compete against other organisms within a single breeding population; those traits (or parts) of organisms that help their possessors to survive and reproduce are favoured by natural selection. It is organismic adaptations that evolve by the sort of natural selection that Darwin postulated.

This view about the nature of adaptations came to the fore in Darwin's dispute with Wallace about sterile hybrids.[8] When organisms from different species manage to produce viable offspring, the offspring frequently are sterile. Why is this? Darwin observed that if hybrids were bound to be sterile, then natural selection would favour individuals who avoided mating with individuals from different species. Interspecific mating would be a poor investment of reproductive capital. However, this does not explain why the hybrids should be sterile, only why hybrid sterility should give rise to certain sorts of mate preference.

Wallace thought that the good of the species could explain why hybrids are sterile. If an organism from species *A* cannot produce fertile offspring when it mates with an individual from species *B*, then species *A* will continue to persist as the distinctive species that it is. In contrast, if the two species are interfertile, then they eventually will mix together and a hybrid species *C* will come to replace *A* and *B*. For Wallace, hybrid sterility evolved because it was good for the species, not because it conferred any benefit on individual organisms.

Darwin rejected this argument in terms of species advantage. He suggested, instead, that hybrid sterility is not an adaptation at all. It is a fortuitous consequence of the various physical differences that distinguish the two species from each other. The individuals in *A* have traits of morphology, physiology, and behaviour that differ from those possessed by the individuals in *B*. These differences evolved in each species because the individuals faced different selection pressures. A consequence of these differences is that hybrids between *A* and *B* often are sterile.

Darwin and Wallace debated this problem at length. Darwin's

attitude towards it exemplified one of his characteristic approaches to the problem of adaptation—if a trait cannot be explained in terms of the advantages it provides to the individuals possessing it, then it cannot be explained by natural selection at all. Although Darwinism is often associated with the slogan 'the good of the species', this in fact is a deeply misleading way to describe Darwin's persistently individualistic approach to natural selection.

There was one context in which Darwin departed from his standing commitment to the organism as the unit of selection. This occurred in his discussion of human morality. In the *Descent of man* (p. 163), he poses the question this way:

> It is extremely doubtful whether the offspring of the more sympathetic and benevolent parents, or of those which were the most faithful to their comrades, would be reared in greater number than the children of selfish and treacherous parents of the same tribe. He who was ready to sacrifice his life, as many a savage has been, rather than betray his comrades, would leave no offspring to inherit his noble nature. The bravest men, who were always willing to come to the front in war, and who freely risked their lives for others would on average perish in larger numbers than other men.

Then Darwin (p. 166) proposes the following selectionist explanation:

> It must not be forgotten that although a high standard of morality gives but a slight or no advantage to each individual man and his children over the other man of the same tribe, yet that an advancement in the standard of morality and an increase in the number of well-endowed men will certainly given an immense advantage to one tribe over another.

When tribes compete against tribes, traits may evolve that are deleterious for the individuals possessing them, though advantageous for the groups in which they occur. In recent biology, such traits have come to be called *altruistic*. Darwinian selection within the confines of a single population cannot lead altruism to evolve; but group selection, in which groups compete against each other within the confines of an ensemble of populations, makes the evolution of altruism at last theoretically possible.[9]

In no other context did Darwin clearly embrace selection at levels higher than that of the individual organism. The Darwinian idea of teleology thus rejects the idea that whole species exist because they provide benefits to human beings. The idea that the entire living world has as its function the aid and comfort of human beings is entirely antithetical to the Darwinian world picture. For the Darwinian, the parts of an earthworm may have a function, but the earthworm itself has no function at all. This is not to deny that the earthworm provides benefits to other species, including human beings. But these benefits are regarded as fortuitous, not as adaptations that now exist because they benefitted other species.[10]

So not only was God not part of Darwin's explanation of the natural order. In addition, the teleological ideas that natural theology had deployed in its explanations of nature were drastically reconstituted. It is not true that God was razored away with all the remaining elements left unchanged. Human beings were no longer central to understanding how nature works. We are but one bud on one branch of the densely bifurcating tree of life.

Freud thought of himself as partners with Galileo and Darwin in the enterprise of deflating human self-love. The earth is not the centre of the universe, human beings do not stand apart from the rest of nature, and the human mind is driven by powerful irrational forces of which human beings generally are unaware. But the Darwinian blow to our *amour propre* is not exhausted by the fact that we have ape ancestors. If the whole living world had the function of serving human ends, we would retain our pride of place, even if our genealogy connected us with other species. Darwinism is not natural theology with natural selection replacing God.

Another aspect of Darwin's concept of evolution contributed to this property of his theory—that it put human beings in their place, so to speak. Darwin's was not the first theory of evolution. For example, earlier in the nineteenth century, Lamarck had proposed a scheme of descent with modification in which a lineage is preprogrammed to move through a sequence of stages. Life begins with simple forms and then gains in complexity. The environment plays a secondary role, in which the circumstances of life can effect small changes (e.g. high leaves can make the giraffe's neck longer). But the principal cause of evolution is endogenous. Its last fruition is that most complex of organisms—human beings.

If all lineages move through the same sequence of life forms, how is one to explain the observed diversity among present day organisms? Lamarck's answer was that different lineages began at different times. Human beings belong to a very old lineage, modern earthworms to a relatively new one. Spontaneous generation allows rudimentary life forms to emerge from inorganic materials. By repeated inputs of this sort, different lineages are begun. Current diversity is the result of different starting times.

Lamarck's evolutionary hypothesis connects human beings with the rest of nature. But human beings none the less remain special. They are last and best. Just as God waited until the final day of creation to produce Adam, so the Lamarckian process must work its way through more rudimentary forms before it can produce human beings. We are what evolution strives for—what it is in evolution's *telos* eventually to achieve.[11]

Darwin's theory of evolution has no such directedness. Natural selection is primarily an exogenous and, so to speak, fortuitous process. If a population happens to possess certain sorts of variants, and if the environment in which it lives happens to entail that some of those variants are fitter, then those will be the variants that happen to increase in frequency. If the range of variation had been different, or if the environmentally generated selection pressures had been different, the end result would have differed as well. Human beings, like everything else in nature, are the result of historical contingency; we are not a preprogrammed inevitability.[12]

I have emphasized some of the discontinuities between Darwin's grand view of nature and that of the natural theology against which he reacted. However, a number of historians of science have shown that Darwin's debt to the natural theologians was substantial.[13] Paley and the tradition of which he was a part posited a beneficent deity who constructed a perfect world; evil is only apparent, or is the regrettable price that God had to pay for a greater good. Organisms are contrivances built by their Creator; they are equipped with the machinery they need to live the lives that God wishes them to lead. The totality of nature exhibits a breathtaking superabundance—it teems with life. This optimistic picture of nature as a whole also applies to human societies. Social hierarchy provides an incentive for those at lower rungs to strive for advancement. And it is only right that advanced industrial countries should extend their power over less developed parts of the globe. Relations within and among societies are as they should be.

These themes in natural theology found parallels in Darwin's nature. Whereas the God of natural theology had created a perfect nature before natural history began to unfold, natural selection, working 'solely by and for the good of each being', insures that 'all corporeal and mental endowments will tend to progress towards perfection' (*Origin*, p. 489). This passage at the end of the *Origin* is followed by one in which Darwin asks the reader to 'contemplate an entangled bank, clothed with many plants of many kinds, with birds singing on the bushes, with various insects flitting about, and with worms crawling through the damp earth.' This natural superabundance gives rise to struggle; progress in nature as a whole is purchased by 'the Extinction of less-improved forms. Thus, from the war of nature, from famine and death, the most exalted object which we are capable of conceiving, namely, the production of the higher animals, directly follows.' Darwin saw 'grandeur in this view of life.' This grandeur did not derive its power from the fact that nature testifies to the perfection of an intelligent Creator. Rather, the majesty of nature consists in the fact that 'from so simple a beginning endless forms most beautiful and wonderful have been, and are being, evolved.'

Paley's approval of inequalities within and among nations also finds its place in Darwin's world view. For example, in the *Descent of man* (p. 135) Darwin connects social hierarchy and European hegemony and argues that they are for the best:

> the inheritance of property by itself is very far from an evil; for without the accumulation of capital the arts could not progress, and it is chiefly through their power that the civilized races have extended and are now everywhere extending their range, so as to take the place of the lower races.

Just as Darwin often took an optimistic view of the improving character of natural selection, so did the struggle for existence as a fact of life within and between nations tend to produce progress. This does not make Darwin a 'vulgar social Darwinist' who applauded every detail of late-nineteenth-century capitalism. Nor does it mean that Darwin saw himself as actively engaged in the enterprise of justifying these social arrangements; they were so natural that the question of justification hardly arose as a major problem. But consistent with all this is the fact that Darwin's view of existing social arrangements was mainly benign.

Although I do not wish to deny this congruence between the God of natural theology and the selective processes in Darwin's nature, there are none the less some points of difference, additional to the ones noted earlier. My point is not to provide a 'balanced' list of similarities and differences, but to isolate central features of Darwin's world view and to note, where appropriate, how they differ from the tradition he inherited.

To begin with, nature is not an *agent*. When God, or a human being, makes a choice, there are the characteristics of the items that might be selected, the criterion that the agent uses, and the action that the agent performs in making the selection. When you go to a restaurant, there are the items on the menu, the preferences you have, and the action you perform in ordering the meal. And, most fundamentally, there is *you*.

In Darwin's concept of natural selection, there need be no agent that does the selecting. If one organism has more efficient lungs than another, the first may be fitter. This organism may survive and reproduce more successfully, and so its advantageous characteristic may become more common in subsequent generations. The organisms and their traits constitute the items on the menu. They do better or worse in the struggle for existence. But there is not, in addition, an agent called 'Nature', which somehow surveys these alternatives and determines which shall live and which shall die.[14]

It is easy to miss this point, because some standard examples of natural selection do involve agents outside of the population under selection. For example, a population of zebras may evolve because some zebras run faster than others, and so are better at evading predators. Here the lions do the selecting and the zebra population evolves. My point is that this is an incidental feature of Darwin's concept. It is gratuitous and possibly misleading to think of 'Nature' as an agent that carries out the process of natural selection.[15]

Another difference between the God of natural theology and Darwinian natural selection is absolutely fundamental to the epistemological status of Darwin's theory. If natural selection had the same consequences for the adaptedness of organisms that a beneficent deity would have, it would have been impossible to use natural observation to distinguish between the hypothesis of natural selection and the hypothesis of intelligent design. If a nature forged by God would look the same as a nature produced by selection, there can be no observational evidence favouring one hypothesis over the other. Those who think that appeal to observation is a naïve and positivist gloss on scientific practice will not be troubled by this implication. But the conclusion must be resisted by those of us who think that Darwin's explanation was better supported by the observations than the hypothesis of separate creation by a beneficent deity.

In the passage quoted earlier from the end of the *Origin*, Darwin describes natural selection as a process by which the traits of organisms 'tend to progress towards perfection'. The first thing to notice about this remark is that organisms are not claimed to be perfect, but to be moving in that direction. It is no part of Darwin's theory that organisms are *unimprovable*. Not only has natural selection modified their characteristics in the past; in addition, the process is at work in the present and will persist into the future. What the God of natural theology did in the six days of creation, Darwin's natural selection achieves in no finite length of time, however large.

Natural selection, in Darwin's conception, is an *improver*. It surveys the variant traits actually present in a population and causes the best of these to gain in frequency. The slogan 'the survival of the fittest' is perhaps a little misleading; it isn't the fittest of all *possible* traits that will evolve, but the fittest of the ones that are *actually* present. So one limitation on the perfecting power of natural selection, which presumably did not constrain the designs of a beneficent deity, was the raw material of variation available as a matter of historical fact. God can actualize the best of all *conceivable* organisms; natural selection is more limited in the degree of perfection it can produce.

Another factor that constrains the power of natural selection to produce perfect organisms is its sequential character. The traits that characterize a present day species are not assembled simultaneously, with natural selection scrutinizing all possible combinations of traits. Rather, each trait evolves against a background of traits that have already evolved in ancestral populations. This means that the present characteristics of a species will not only suit it more or less to the environment it inhabits; in addition, the characteristics will include indications of the traits that its ancestors possessed. The ensemble of traits may be useful to the present day organisms possessing them, but they also will retain the marks of the historical process from which they emerged.

An important example of this sort is the existence of rudimentary organs. In the *Origin* (p. 453), Darwin notes that if one reflects on such characteristics, one 'must be struck with astonishment; for the same reasoning power which tells us plainly that most parts and organs are exquisitely adapted for certain purposes, tells us with equal plainness that these rudimentary or atrophied organs, are imperfect and useless.' A benevolent God would not design organisms with such characteristics. But, as Darwin remarks, 'on my view of descent with modification, the origin of rudimentary organs is simple.'

Even traits that subserve a function will show signs of their history; they were not designed from scratch, but were the result of 'tinkering' with previous characteristics.[16] A nice example that illustrates this Darwinian idea is the panda's thumb. Pandas are vegetarians subsisting on bamboo. They run the bamboo branch between their main paw and a spur of bone (a 'thumb') that juts out from the wrist. This extremely inefficient method of preparing food would not have been the arrangement chosen by an intelligent designer. But given that pandas are descended from carnivorous bears, their thumbs can be understood as modifications of ancestral structures.[17]

Darwin also notes that there are facts about the similarities and differences among species that are quite puzzling on the hypothesis of separate creation by an intelligent designer, but which become readily intelligible if one adopts the joint hypothesis of the tree of life and natural selection. There are species that live in very similar habitats, which none the less are quite different in various ways. Blind fish live in caves around the world. There are traits that they have in common, but there also are many prominent differences. If God created each species to fit into its environment, why are these species so different from each other? On the other hand, if the ancestors of these different species were themselves quite different, then it makes sense that the descendants should retain some of these differences.

Absolutely perfect adaptation entails a one-to-one correspondence between traits and environments. If two species differ with respect to some trait, this must be because each trait is optimal for the environment in which it occurs, and the environments are relevantly different. Conversely, if two species share some trait, this must be because there is a commonality between their environments such that what is optimal for one environment also is optimal for the other. The idea of the tree of life provides a quite different kind of explanation for similarities and differences among species, one which undercuts the one-to-one correspondence that is a consequence of the idea of perfect adaptation. Species may be similar because they are closely related; they may differ because their ancestors were different. These entailments are orthogonal to the implications of perfect adaptation.

Darwin emphasized the power of natural selection to produce the adaptations we observe in nature. But in making this argument, he had to be careful not to go too far. For if natural selection *perfectly* adapted organisms to their environments, their genealogical relationships to each other would be invisible. Darwin expresses this idea in the following passage from the *Origin* (p. 427):

> On my view of characters being of real importance for classification, only in so far as they reveal descent, we can clearly understand why analogical or adaptive characters, although of the utmost importance to the welfare of the being, are almost valueless to the systematist. For animals, belonging to two most distinct lines of descent, may readily become adapted to similar conditions, and thus assume a close external resemblance; but such resemblances will not reveal—will rather tend to conceal their blood-relationship to their proper lines of descent.

The tree of life and natural selection are the two halves of Darwin's theory of evolution, but their relationship to each other is a paradoxical one: the more powerful natural selection is, the less evidence there will be to reconstruct the tree of life. Darwin therefore had to walk a fine line—natural selection had to be *just powerful enough*. Were natural selection too weak a force, it would be incapable of explaining the adaptive contrivances we find in nature. But if natural selection were limitless in its power to perfect, the tree of life would be no better supported by natural observation than the hypothesis of special creation by a beneficent deity.[18]

Although Darwinian natural selection acts on differences among individual organisms, a principal goal of Darwin's theory was to explain the origin of *species*. It is clear enough how natural selection can modify the characteristics of an existing species. But what role does the process play in the proliferation of species that is required by the tree of life idea? If the genealogy of life has the topology of a tree, then a single ancestral species must be able to produce more than one descendant species. What is required is that species split into parts, which themselves turn into distinct species. Natural selection can participate in *cladogenesis* (the branching of lineages) just as it can be the cause of *anagenesis* (the modification of existing lineages). Natural selection produces new species when there is selection for one suite of traits in one part of the ancestral species and selection for another suite of characters in the other. The parts of the old species diverge from each other, until the descendants of one part cannot be counted as conspecific with the descendants of the other.

Darwin's idea of natural selection was able to address the problem of the origin of species only by supposing that species boundaries are not immutable. This went against a very strong biological tradition that argued that there are limits beyond which a species cannot be pushed. That a species at a given time contains variation was recognized from the earliest days of biological theorizing. The question was whether a species moving through time could manifest much more variation than it displays at a given time. Even the most detailed static snapshot of the variation present at a time does not settle definitively this dynamical question.

No one in Darwin's day directly observed the birth of a new species. Rather, Darwin's conjecture rested in part on an extrapolation from the smaller scale changes that had been observed. If artificial selection[19] was able to create new varieties within species in the relatively short time frame of human history, then natural selection, occurring during larger reaches of time, should be able to produce changes of even greater magnitude.[20] If varieties are simply incipient species, as Darwin maintained, then natural selection will encounter no impediments as it gradually but persistently makes over a lineage.

It greatly facilitated the case that Darwin wished to argue that he abandoned an essentialist conception of species. Essentialism requires that each species be definable by listing properties that are separately necessary and jointly sufficient for an organism to belong to the species. Though there may be dispute over the details of how a particular species should be defined, the effect of adopting this framework is to force one to look for characteristics unique to a species that all members of the species share. Differences among tigers, or among human beings, are viewed as merely accidental, and as having little theoretical significance.[21]

Darwin did not announce that this essentialist program was bankrupt. Rather, he quietly abandoned it and focused his attention instead on the very opposite kind of characteristic. What was significant theoretically for Darwinian processes was not the similarities that occur within a species, but the differences that separate conspecifics from each other. Natural selection acts on variation. Perhaps as a result of selection, the organisms in a species may come to share a trait that happens to be unique to them. What causes evolution by natural selection is *differences*; a possible, though not inevitable, effect of this evolution is *uniformity* within species. This view stood on its head the roles that Aristotle had assigned to similarities and differences within a species. For Aristotle, all members of a given species share the same essence. It is not that tigers all have stripes, or that all are carnivorous, or that all have four legs. Rather, being a four-legged striped carnivore is the natural state towards which all tigers tend. This phenotype is like the target at which the archer aims. Interferences with natural development can deflect individuals from attaining their natural states. Variation among tigers is due to accidents of development; what tigers have in common is a common nature. Here the variation found within the species is an *effect* (of imperfect development); that which all tigers have in common (their common nature) is a causal factor in the development of each and every tiger.[22]

Statistical thinking is now so deeply ingrained in biology and in the rest of science that it is difficult to fathom the hold that this essentialist picture had on scientific thought. A present day population biologist will characterize a species by the variation it contains and will be entirely untroubled if there is no trait that all and only the members of the species share. Modern biology shrugs off as unmotivated and metaphysical the idea that variation is a veil that must be swept aside if the biologist is to see the true nature of things. Yet this contemporary attitude towards variation has its history; it emerged as an intelligible approach to the study of nature only during the nineteenth century. The normal curve, as we now call it, was once called the Law of Error. Early models of the distribution of variation, like those of Laplace and Quetelet, were based on the archer metaphor in which a central tendency is subject to random interferences.[23] Statistics kicked away this ladder once it had been used to leave essentialism behind. Not least of the revolutionary achievements of Darwin's theory of natural selection was that it contributed to this project by postulating a process in which variation is of the essence, and uniformity only a possible byproduct.

ACKNOWLEDGEMENT

I am grateful to Thomas Browman, Gregg Mitman, and Lynn Nyhart for useful discussion.

NOTES

1. Here I am indebted to Frank M. Turner's 'The secularization of the social vision of British natural theology', unpublished.

2. Robert Richards, *Darwin and the emergence of evolutionary theories of mind and behavior* (University of Chicago Press, 1987), pp. 77–8. See also the discussion in Neil Gillespie's *Charles Darwin and the problem of creation* (University of Chicago Press 1979).
3. For an illuminating survey of Darwin's range of scientific interests, see Michael Ghiselin, *The triumph of the Darwinian method* (University of California Press 1969).
4. I argue that some of Hume's criticisms of the design argument rest on an indefensibly narrow inductivism in my *Core questions in philosophy* (Macmillan 1991), pp. 49–55.
5. I discuss whether and why the parsimoniousness of a hypothesis should be taken as a reason to think that it is true in my *Reconstructing the past: parsimony, evolution, and inference* (MIT Press 1988).
6. Albert Einstein, 'On the electrodynamics of moving bodies'. Reprinted in A. Einstein *et al.*, *The principle of relativity* (Dover 1952).
7. I discuss the current biological controversy about the units of selection, as well as its historical context, in my *The nature of selection* (MIT Press 1984), Chapters 7–9.
8. Here I am indebted to Michael Ruse, 'Charles Darwin and group selection', *Annals of Science*, **37** (1980) 615–30.
9. For further discussion of the conceptual requirements for altruism to evolve by group selection, see my 'What is evolutionary altruism?', in *New essays on philosophy and biology*, ed. B. Linsky and M. Matthen (Canadian Journal of Philosophy Suppl. Vol. 14), University of Calgary Press 1988), pp. 75–99.
10. Darwin sometimes says that natural selection can act for the good of the group. However, the examples he discusses of natural selection, except for the one just described, usually admit of interpretation in terms of individual benefit. It is arguable that the distinction between individual and group benefit was not always crystal clear in Darwin's writings (nor has it always been in subsequent biology). Typically, the group benefit that results from an adaptation can be regarded as a fortuitous consequence; the trait evolved because of the individual benefits it provided. However, on the idea that a given species might exist because it provides benefits for another, Darwin is entirely unequivocal. The following passage from the *Origin* (p. 87) is characteristic: 'in social animals it [selection] will adapt the structure of each individual for the benefit of the community; if each in consequence profits by the selected change. What natural selection cannot do, is to modify the structure of one species, without giving it any advantage, for the good of another species; and though statements to this effect

may be found in works of natural history, I cannot find one case which will bear investigation.'

11. Lamarck did allow that stages beyond human beings might be possible. But this speculative possibility does not undercut the idea that in the world as we find it, all other life forms are transitory stages that evolution must move through in order to reach the human form of life.
12. Many nineteenth-century German biologists objected to this element in Darwin's theory; although they accepted the tree of life idea, they thought that the fortuitousness of natural selection contradicted the constraint that biology is governed by laws. See the discussion of the history of the idea of *laws of form* in Stephen Jay Gould's *Ontogeny and phylogeny* (Harvard University Press 1977).
13. See, for example, W. Cannon, 'The bases of Darwin's achievement: a reevaluation', *Victorian Studies*, **5** (1961) 109–34; Dov Ospovat, *The development of Darwin's theory* (Cambridge University Press 1981); Robert Young, *Darwin's metaphor: nature's place in Victorian culture* (Cambridge University Press 1985); Peter Bowler, *The Non-Darwinian revolution* (Johns Hopkins University Press 1988); Robert Richards, *op. cit.*
14. This point is a pleasant one to make in the Oxford of Gilbert Ryle.
15. Just as selection is a process without an agent, so adaptation is a process without a subject. Darwinian natural selection creates a better adapted organism, but no (token) organism need change its traits in the process. Organisms can be static, even though the population of organisms changes. No single organism need 'adapt to its environment' for an adaptation to arise. Nor can one say that the *population* is adapting in this process, since the traits that evolve are good for organisms, not for the populations in which they occur. See Elliott Sober, *The nature of selection* (MIT Press 1984), pp. 147–54, and Richard Lewontin, 'Darwin's revolution,' *New York Review of Books*, **30** (1983) 21–7, for discussion of the distinction between variational and developmental theories of change.
16. This apt phrase is from Francois Jacob, 'Evolution and tinkering', *Science*, **196** (1977) 1161–6.
17. This example is due to Stephen Jay Gould, *The panda's thumb*, (Norton 1980).
18. A modern example of this line of argument is the idea that the near universality of the genetic code strongly supports the hypothesis that all life is related. A crucial element in this inference is the (plausible)

assumption that the code is *arbitrary*. If only one code were physically possible, or if the code we find in nature were fitter than the alternatives, the evidence for common ancestry provided by the common code would be less compelling.

19. It is interesting to observe how Darwin uses the terms 'artificial' and 'natural' as modifiers of his term 'selection'. Plant and animal breeders engage in artificial selection when they intentionally modify the characteristics of a population of organisms. Natural selection yields the same result, but without the intervention of intelligent planning. Darwin, in this instance, acquiesced in the terminological convention that separates nature from artifice. However, this belies the fact that he totally subverted the theory on which this convention rests. For Darwin, artificial selection was an experiment that people had conducted without realizing that they were doing so. The subject of the experiment was natural selection. The farm was a laboratory, modelling processes at work in the wild. Given this relationship between human work and the workings of nature, the terms 'natural' and 'artificial' selection do not mark a difference of any theoretical importance. A physicist in a laboratory may investigate electricity, but it would be absurd to say that there are two kinds of electricity—artificial and natural.
20. For discussion of Darwin's investigations into artificial selection and their influence on his evolutionary ideas, see Michael Ruse, 'Charles Darwin and artificial selection', *Journal of the History of Ideas*, **36** (1975) 339–50.
21. For discussion of the influence of essentialism on pre-Darwinian biology, see David Hull 'The effect of essentialism on taxonomy: 2000 years of stasis', *British Journal for the Philosophy of Science*, **15** (1965) 314–26; **16** (1965) 1–18.
22. I flesh out this summary statement of Artistotle's 'natural state model' for accounting for variation within a kind in my *The nature of selection* (MIT Press 1984), pp.155–70. The contrast drawn here between Darwin and Aristotle is an elaboration of Ernst Mayr's 'Typological versus population thinking' (*Evolution and the diversity of life* (Harvard University Press 1976), pp. 26–9) and of Richard Lewontin's introduction to his *The genetic basis of evolutionary change* (Columbia University Press 1974).
23. See Stephen Stigler, *The history of statistics: the measurement of uncertainty before 1900* (Harvard University Press 1986). Laplace discussed variation in multiple measurements of a single physical quantity in terms of random errors occluding one's perception of the

unique true value. However, Quetelet applied the same format to explaining the variation in girth found within a regiment of soldiers. Whereas the former approach sounds quite natural to the modern ear, the latter sounds quite bizarre. It is a testimonial to the power of the natural state model that Quetelet's ideas could have had scientific currency.

5

The modern physicist's view of nature

ROGER PENROSE
Mathematical Institute, University of Oxford

I have been asked to describe the modern physicist's view of nature, and you may very reasonably ask: what right does a mere mathematician have to pontificate on what he believes to be the picture of nature held by physicists? Perhaps it would be best if you are to take my remarks as presenting the *mathematician's* view of the modern physicist's view of nature, or rather, one particular mathematician's view of the modern physicist's view of nature. None the less, it is certainly true that modern physics could not exist without mathematics, nor, indeed, without mathematics of ever-increasing sophistication. This has been particularly true of work done over the past ten years or so, but it has been true, also over the entire history of the development of successful physical theory from early Greek times until the present day. Perhaps, after all, it is not so unreasonable for a mathematician to take over the task of describing the physicist's view of nature.

Let me begin by attempting to put the physicist's achievements in some kind of perspective. First of all, I think that it is important for us not to get too carried away by their excitement about whatever fashionable ideas happen to be taking their interest at any one moment. For the physicists themselves, on the other hand, it is not at all inappropriate that they should get carried away. Their own enthusiasm is a vital ingredient for real progress in fundamental physics. Physics is an area where the mathematics can get extremely difficult at times and is frequently very tedious, so that a physicist's feeling that goals (and perhaps rich rewards) are close at hand is essential for progress. For the rest of us (and for the physicists, also, when in their more reflective moods), it is necessary to be more circumspect. Let us try to assess the status of the physicists' achievements over the whole of history.

It should be pointed out that some of these achievements have indeed been truly remarkable. The best of the physicist's theories have acquired a status unmatched in any other science (where by the term 'science', I do not include mathematics). Such theories I refer to as SUPERB. To qualify as SUPERB, it is not necessary for the theory to apply without refutation to the phenomena of the world, but its range and accuracy must, in some appropriate sense, be *phenomenal*. The way that I am using the term 'SUPERB', it is a quite extraordinary fact that there are any theories in this category at all. I do not believe that any basic theory in any other science could properly qualify as SUPERB. The only possible exception might be Darwin and Wallace's theory of natural selection (as amended by Mendel), but even that theory, for all its power and scope, and for all the insights that it gives us into the workings of the biological world, perhaps does not quite achieve the precision in numerical accuracy that would allow it to qualify, in the terms that I am laying down, for the SUPERB category. In saying this, I am in no way being disrespectful to the theory of natural selection. On the contrary, I am simply emphasizing the extraordinary accuracy and scope of those physical theories that to indeed qualify as SUPERB.

Which are the SUPERB theories? Let me list these as I see them:

(1) Euclidean geometry
(2) classical statics
(3) Newtonian dynamics
(4) Maxwellian electrodynamics
(5) special relativity
(6) general relativity
(7) thermodynamics
(8) quantum mechanics
(9) quantum electrodynamics.

I shall give a brief description of each of these, indicating why it should indeed be considered as a SUPERB physical theory, and then touch upon the rest of mainstream physics, all of which belongs to the remaining categories, which I label USEFUL or TENTATIVE (or perhaps even MISGUIDED).

EUCLIDEAN GEOMETRY

Let us begin with Euclidean geometry. This is simply the subject of 'geometry' that we learn something of at school. Why do I refer to Euclidean geometry as a *physical* theory rather than a branch of mathematics? Of course it is mathematics as well: the classical example of a deductive system, where axioms are laid down to begin with and hosts of propositions are then derived from them in step-by-step logical ways. But the reason for the very choice of axioms in the first place is that they agree extraordinarily closely with the physical notion of a 'point' as the tiniest of particles and of a 'straight line' as a ray of light—or else as a line attached to a rigid body (say a ruler), where the line can be moved along itself and independently turned about itself. If we had had no familiarity with such physical straight lines, with rigidity, or with tiny point-like specks of physical matter, then Euclid's geometry would not seem so 'natural' or 'obvious' to us. The seeming self-evidence of the Euclidean axioms arises from the fact that we inhabit a physical space occupied by rigid physical objects that behave in a very accurate way according to the laws of Euclid's geometry. It is initially the structure of the physical world, not just mathematics, that suggests to us the axioms that we should choose; it is mathematics, on the other hand, that is concerned with deductions that can be made from those axioms.

There are two distinct ways in which the ideal Euclidean theory of geometry can fail to describe the physical world precisely. The first of these is that physical bodies need not be precisely rigid; nor can we expect to find, in nature, precisely straight physical lines of zero thickness or tiny specks or marks that are precisely pointlike. Normally one does not regard this as an essential obstacle to our taking the geometry of 'actual' space to *be* Euclidan. We may regard physical objects as having finite extension, and also as being deformable, so long as these extensions and deformations are things that take place *in* Euclidean space and can be measured and unambiguously described, according to an appropriate theory, in terms of standard Euclidean concepts of distance and angle—in short, so long as we can, in principle, make the appropriate *corrections* that tell us how we must expect our actual physical objects to deviate from the physical ideals of 'pointlike', 'straight', or 'rigid'. Accordingly, we think of 'space' itself as having a precisely Euclidean structure, the physical objects themselves perhaps falling short of this ideal in one way or another.

The second way in which Euclidean geometry might fall short of complete accuracy is more subtle. There are actually kinds of geometry other than Euclidean geometry that are mathematically possible. One of these, for example, is what is called *Lobachevskian* (or hyperbolic) geometry. Lobachevskian geometry satisfies all the axioms of Euclidean geometry except for 'Euclid's fifth postulate'—with the implication that in Lobachevskian geometry there will be more than one straight line through a given point that is parallel to another given straight line (not through the point). In Fig. 1, I have provided an Escher print giving a representation of this geometry (within a portion of a Euclidean plane). All the black fish are to be regarded as congruent and so also are all the white fish. The outer circle denotes 'infinity', and the entire Lobachevskian plane is represented as the interior of this circle. The Lobachevskian straight lines are represented as circles meeting the boundary circle at right angles. We can also think of Lobachevskian *three*-space as being represented in a similar way, except that the space is now represented as the interior of a sphere instead of a circle. (These representations were found by Poincaré—although I am told that Beltrami had known about them many years earlier.) Now it could turn out that the most appropriate concept of 'actual physical space' is not Euclidean at all, but it might be some other kind of geometry, such as the Lobachevskian geometry just described. We might still try to imagine that the underlying space is 'actually' Euclidean, and that any deviations from Euclidean geometry that *real* physical bodies might experience could be accounted for by taking the 'corrections' point of

Fig. 1 Escher's depiction of Lobachevskian space. (Think of all the black fish as congruent and all the white fish as congruent.)

view, as described above. However, this may not be at all appropriate. In the first place, deviations from the supposed 'actual Euclidean underlying space' that real physical bodies would need to acquire can get unreasonably large, perhaps getting larger and larger and farther into the distance that these bodies are examined, so that the supposed underlying geometry begins to have little relationship with the (approximate) geometry described by the real bodies themselves. A second reason for the inappropriateness of such a concept of 'underlying Euclidean geometry' is that there may be no uniqueness about it when it does not accord closely with the geometry respected by real physical objects. There may be a clear sense in which the most appropriate physical geometry is not Euclidean after all.

How well does Euclid's geometry in fact describe the physical world? It turns out that when we have taken into account all the 'corrections' that need to be made, there still remains a deviation in the behaviour of physical objects, from the underlying Euclidean ideal. This deviation is utterly tiny, however, and in total it would not amount to more than the diameter of an atom of hydrogen in a region a metre or so across in any normal part of space. But the fact that deviations do occur emphasizes that Euclidean geometry is indeed a falsifiable physical theory and not just a piece of mathematics. The extraordinary accuracy of this theory, and the scope and power of its applicability to the physical world gives it an undoubted place among the SUPERB theories. The fact that deviations do exist in no way bars it from membership. (We shall see with the other SUPERB theories, that the existence of tiny deviations is the rule rather than the exception.)

The deviations from Euclid's geometry are in fact accounted for by anther SUPERB theory, general relativity, which we shall be coming to shortly. But before we move on, I should point out that there is a fundamental ingredient of Euclidean geometry, namely the concept of a *real number*, that was introduced, in effect by Eudoxos in the fourth century BC, that has remained with us, unchanged to the present day, as an essential ingredient of *all* successful physical theories including general relativity. (Real numbers are, in modern everyday terms, what we would describe using infinite decimal expansions—although Eudoxos, in his day, used a different method.) Whether the real number will retain this essential status in future SUPERB theories remains to be seen, however.

CLASSICAL STATICS

There was another great scientific achievement established largely by the ancient Greeks, although a little later than Euclidean geometry. This was the theory of *statics*, due mainly to Archimedes (287–212 BC) and Pappos (late third century AD), and also

Simon Stevin (*c.* 1548–*c.* 1620). This theory described objects in equilibrium (i.e. balanced, so that there is no motion), and it included the law of the lever and properties of bodies suspended in fluids, including the concepts of pressure and force, etc. The accuracy of this theory must have been very great, especially considering the antiquity of its basic ideas, and bearing in mind the comparatively primitive means that were available to check them. The ancients could construct such an accurate body of laws largely because they were able to find a number of ingenious and clearcut mathematical arguments, starting from certain 'obvious' principles (such as symmetry properties, and the non-existence of a *perpetuum mobile*). We do not now tend to think of classical statics as a physical theory in its own right, because it has been subsumed by the more general scheme of Newtonian dynamics. But I have chosen to list it separately here because, for some eighteen centuries, it stood independently as a profound testament to the power of mathematical theory in accurately describing the physical world.

NEWTONIAN DYNAMICS

The main thing that was lacking in early Greek science was a good understanding of the laws governing bodies in *motion*. They appear to have believed that the laws governing the motions of celestial bodies were quite different from those which controlled the motions of bodies on earth. Their ideas about earth-bound motions were very inaccurate. However, they did have accurate empirical knowledge of the motions of celestial bodies, and they formulated a family of laws to describe such motion, now referred to as the *Ptolemaic* system (due, in successive refinements, to Eudoxos, Hipparchos, and Ptolemy). This system described the movement, around the earth, of the planets, the moon, and the sun, in terms of complicated compositions of circular motions. It provided a useful scheme of quite creditable accuracy and predictive power, though it became more and more over-complicated as the need for greater accuracy increased. It was a wonderful classical example of a theory belonging to the category that I am referring to as USEFUL (for about twenty centuries, in fact!). The work of Copernicus and Kepler changed that picture considerably, and it provided another USEFUL theory, according to which the planets move, instead, about the sun, in elliptical orbits with the sun at one focus.

The system of dynamics initiated by Galileo in about 1600 and completed by Newton in 1687 changed things dramatically. Now, the same laws were seen to apply here on earth as governed the motions of celestial bodies. Moreover, instead of having a merely descriptive scheme in which the orbits described by the planets' motions were thought of as geometrical things in their entirety, we were presented with a full *dynamics*, where laws were given determining how the motion of each body changed from moment to moment—i.e. how each body *accelerated*—in terms of the locations and nature of all other bodies. Newton's dynamical laws, together with specific laws of force such as the inverse square law of gravitation, gave an incredibly detailed and accurate account of the motions of bodies. Now it was possible not only to *deduce* Kepler's elliptical motion from more primitive dynamical laws, but innumerable corrections to this motion could be worked out and found to be in very close accordance with what was actually observed. The agreement, in Newton's day, between theory and observation was to something like one part in a thousand; today, that agreement is to better than one part in ten million. Certainly Newtonian dynamics must qualify as SUPERB!

It should be pointed out that the much earlier SUPERB theory of Euclidean geometry is an essential part of Newtonian dynamics, this geometry forming the background to all Newtonian descriptions. Moreover, not only has the SUPERB theory of classical statics been subsumed into Newtonian dynamics, but so also has Kepler's USEFUL theory of planetary motion; while, on the other hand, that other USEFUL theory, the Ptolemaic system, has suffered the opposite fate: it has faded away altogether.

MAXWELLIAN ELECTRODYNAMICS

Classical Newtonian theory is concerned with the motions of *particles*, and a single particle is something that can be described by a small finite number of parameters (three to determine its position in space and three more to fix its velocity, or momentum; and one may require a few more for its mass and, say electric charge and perhaps radius and spin). Classical particles are not sufficient for the description of nature, however. Since the time of Faraday (1791–1867) and Maxwell (1831–79) it has become clear that electric and magnetic fields are things that must be considered as having physical existence in their own right, and cannot be regarded as merely appendages to the physically existing particles, as had been possible with the 'gravitational field' of Newtonian theory, which can be regarded as merely providing 'bookkeeping' for the various forces on the particles. The Faraday–Maxwell theory explains the phenomenon of *light* as a propagation through space of disembodied electric and magnetic fields. Such electromagnetic waves can carry energy and information from one place to another at the speed c that light indeed achieves. Not only is visible light now understood in these terms, but a host of other phenomena are explained and predicted on the basis of this theory, such as radio waves and X-rays. Electromagnetic fields must be regarded as just as 'real' as particles themselves.

Maxwell provided a beautiful family of equations to describe the behaviour of electromagnetic fields. Maxwell's equations are examples of what are called *partial* differential equations, which distinguishes them from the *ordinary* differential equations that arise in the Newtonian descriptions for the motions of individual particles. This difference arises largely because Maxwell's field requires a (continuous) *infinite* number of parameters in order to describe it completely, as opposed to the finite number that is needed for Newton's particles.

Maxwell's theory is accurately valid over an extraordinary range, reaching inwards to the tiny scale of atoms and subatomic particles, and outwards, also, to that of galaxies, some 10^{36} times larger. (At the very small end of the scale, Maxwell's equations must be amended appropriately by combining them with the rules of quantum mechanics.) Maxwellian dynamics, also, must qualify as SUPERB.

SPECIAL RELATIVITY

One of the most important properties of the dynamical theory of Galileo and Newton is that it satisfies a *relativity* principle. The dynamical laws remain unchanged if the reference frame to which they are referred is replaced by another frame in uniform (i.e. non-accelerating, non-rotating) motion with respect to the first. Thus, no local experiment can distinguish a state of uniform motion from the state of rest. (This property is essential, in order that the Copernican heliocentric viewpoint can make dynamical sense.)

A fundamental difficulty arises, however, when Maxwell's electromagnetic theory is adjoined to Newtonian dynamics. Maxwell's equations do not share the invariance properties relevant to the relativity principle of Galileo and Newton. (The simple reason for this is that the speed of light c is built into Maxwell's equations, so that light propagation has an unambiguous velocity in the original reference frame. With respect to a moving reference frame, the speed of light would be diminished in one direction and increased in the opposite direction.) Maxwell's theory on its own, however, does satisfy a relativity principle, though the transformation laws are different from those of Newtonian dynamics. Lorentz, Poincaré, and Einstein showed how Newtonian theory must be modified in order that this new relativity principle can apply to physical systems generally. The theory thus obtained is called *special relativity*.

The most fundamental difference between the laws of special relativity and those of Newtonian dynamics is in the way in which *time* is to be understood. In Newtonian theory, there is a universal time, describable in terms of a single real parameter t. It makes invariant sense to say, of two spatially separated events, whether or not they occur at the same time. In special relativity, this is no longer true. Two events P and Q may be judged to be simultaneous with respect to one reference frame, while with respect to a second one, moving uniformly with respect to the first, one of P or Q may be judged as occurring earlier than the other.

In order to understand this curious behaviour, it is best to take a *space–time* viewpoint rather than a merely spatial one. In a space–time picture, the different points are to represent different *events*, where an event is something with a precise ('instantaneous') temporal location as well as a precise spatial location. Since the picture has to include time as well as space, it has to be *four*-dimensional; but for visualization purposes, it is usual to suppress one (or two) of the spatial dimensions. First, let us see how the relativity of Galileo and Newton can be understood in space–time terms. In Fig. 2, I have drawn a picture of Galilean space–time (with one spatial dimension suppressed). The different horizontal slices through the picture are to represent the whole of (Euclidean) space at various different times. Thus, two events are *simultaneous* if they lie on the same horizontal slice. Time is depicted as increasing upwards in the picture, so that if two events are not simultaneous, then the later one is the one depicted as lying on the higher of the two horizontal planes. The principle of Galilean relativity manifests itself in the fact that we do not make a natural association between the points of one horizontal plane and the points of the next one (so we do not draw in vertical lines indicat-

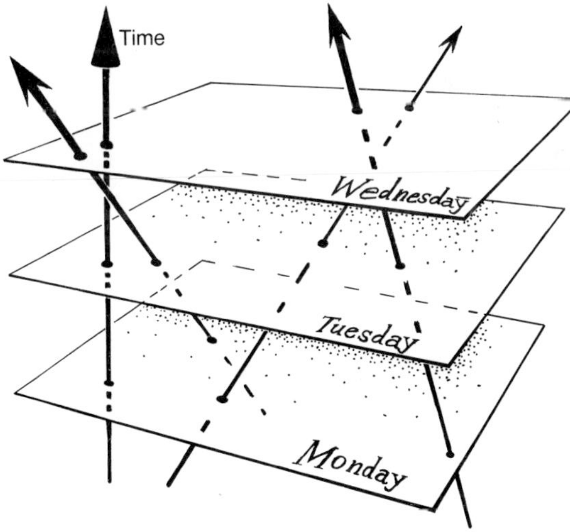

Fig. 2 Galilean space–time: particles in uniform motion are depicted as straight lines.

ing which point in space at one particular time is supposed to be identified with some particular point at another time). This illustrates the fact that there is no natural 'state of rest' distinguished from all other uniform motions. The Galilean relativity transformations (which leave the dynamical laws unchanged) correspond to 'shearing motions' of space–time, in which the horizontal planes are slid along one another, but in such a way that the straight lines in the picture (representing the histories of inertially moving particles) remain straight.

In special relativity the picture is different. We must adopt a space–time geometry that was put forward by Minkowski in 1908. There is no absolute concept of simultaneity, so we now have no horizontal planes. Instead, we must depict the *light cones*, which represent the histories of the flashes of light emitted from various events depicted in the space–time (see Fig. 3(a)). There is a concept of time that is *not* now universal, but which depends upon the motion of the object that is measuring or experiencing that time. The history, or *world-line*, of a particle—which is a curve in space–time—carries a measure of 'length', called its *Minkowskian length*, that describes the passage of time that the particle experiences. Minkowskian length is closely analogous to Euclidean length, but there is a sign difference in the defining expression,

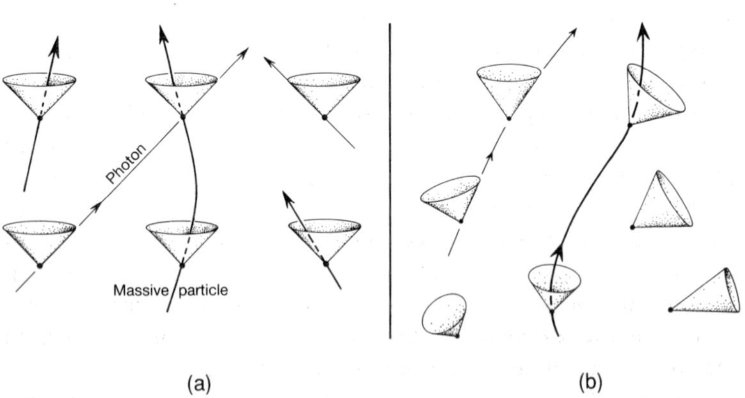

Fig. 3 Space–time pictures in relativity. The light cones at various points are depicted. (a) Minkowskian geometry; (b) general relativity.

which implies that this 'length' gets shorter and shorter as the slope of the line approaches that of the light cone (i.e. 'moving clocks run slow'), becoming actually zero *on* the light cone. Thus photons (particles of light—which we may think of as tiny localized regions of electromagnetic oscillation) experience no passage of time at all between the event of emission and the event of absorption. Any material (massive) particle must have its world-line constrained to lie *inside* the light cones. It turns out that the straight world-lines—describing inertially moving particles—are curves that *maximize* (rather than minimize) the Minkowskian length.

The transformations of special relativity (called Lorentz or Poincaré transformations) are those that preserve the Minkowskian length. They correspond to changing from the reference system of one inertially moving observer to that of another. The planes (actually Euclidean three-spaces) that appear to represent 'space' to one such observer, at each different time, can be drawn as a family of horizontal slices through the space–time picture. These are his *simultaneous* spaces. When we pass to a second inertial observer, we find that his simultaneous spaces are 'tilted' with respect to those of the first observer, so the concept of 'simultaneity' differs between the two. In particular, there could be two events R and Q, where according to one observer, R precedes Q, while for the other, Q precedes R (see Fig. 4).

Normally, we think of these differences in temporal ordering to be very tiny, or to be relevant only for relative velocities that are

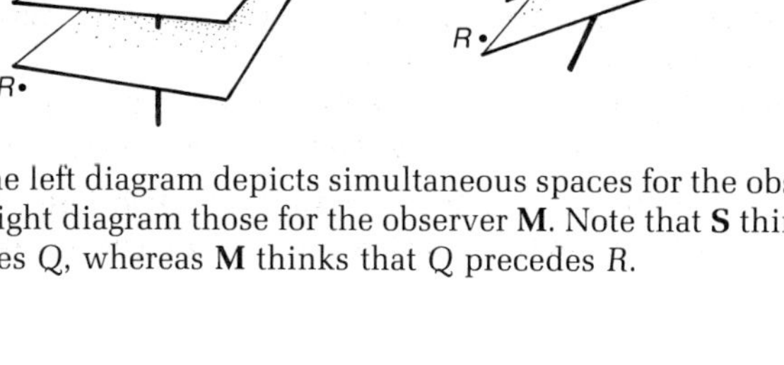

Fig. 4 The left diagram depicts simultaneous spaces for the observer **S** and the right diagram those for the observer **M**. Note that **S** thinks that *R* precedes *Q*, whereas **M** thinks that *Q* precedes *R*.

close to the speed of light. However, it is worth pointing out that even for very modest relative velocities, significant differences in time ordering will occur for events at great distances. Imagine two people walking slowly past each other in the street. The difference between two events on the Andromeda galaxy (which is the closest large galaxy to our own Milky Way, being some 2×10^{19} kilometres distant from us), that would be judged by the two people to be simultaneous with the moment that they pass one another, could amount to a difference of several days (see Fig. 5). For one

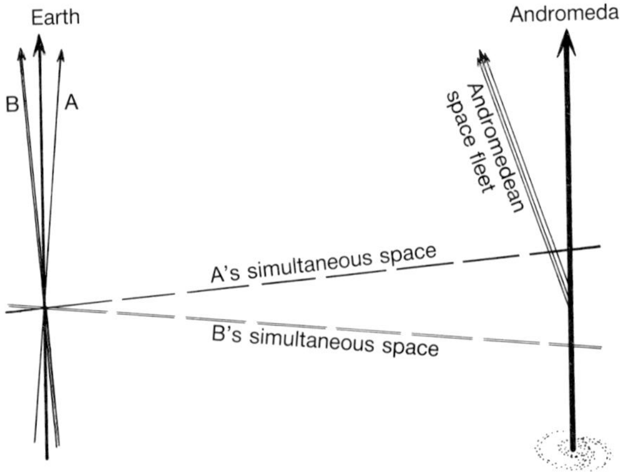

Fig. 5 Two people A and B walk slowly past each other, but they have differing views as to whether the Andromedean space fleet had been launched at the moment they pass each other.

of the people, the space fleet launched with the intent to wipe out all life on the planet Earth is already on its way; while for the other, the very decision as to whether to launch that fleet has not yet even been made!

Despite all this strangeness, special relativity is a phenomenally accurate theory. The Minkowskian length has been confirmed in many different ways as the 'time' that clocks or particles actually measure or respond to. The most direct verification of this comes from time measurements made by very accurate clocks carried in aeroplanes. These clocks 'run slow' in a way that is in precise agreement with relativity (though when the effects of gravity become important, some additional effects of *general* relativity must also be taken into account; see next section). Even more precise measurements come from observations that are being made all the time in connection with particle physics where, for example, the decay lifetimes of fast-moving cosmic rays are enormously extended with respect to a reference frame fixed on the earth. Einstein's $E = mc^2$ (which is an essential part of special relativity, arising when the Lorentz transformation laws are applied to the concepts of energy, momentum, and mass) has been confirmed in many detailed ways, to great numerical accuracy. Special relativity is undoubtedly a SUPERB theory.

GENERAL RELATIVITY

The accuracy of special relativity is not perfect, however, and tiny discrepancies arise when the phenomenon of gravity becomes important. These discrepancies are admirably accounted for by Einstein's *general relativity*. Again, we must adopt a space–time view, rather than a purely spatial one, but now the picture does not have the uniformity of Mikowski's space–time picture of special relativity, as depicted in Fig. 3. Instead, the geometry is more complicated, though it resembles Minkowskian geometry on a small scale approaching it more and more closely as the scale gets smaller. Thus, as before, we have light cones emanating from the various events in the space–time, representing the histories of light flashes originating at these events. Material particles are constrained to have their world-lines lying within these cones, whilst photons' world-lines lie along the cones. However, the cones are now not distributed in a uniform manner (see Fig. 3b), but are 'bent away' from their standard Minkowskian positions. We must think of these cones as marked on some kind of deformable medium (like a rubber sheet) so that any one of the cones can be moved, if desired, into a standard vertical position—so, locally, the space–time geometry resembles that of Minkowski. But it turns out not to be possible to distort the picture as a whole, in this way, so that

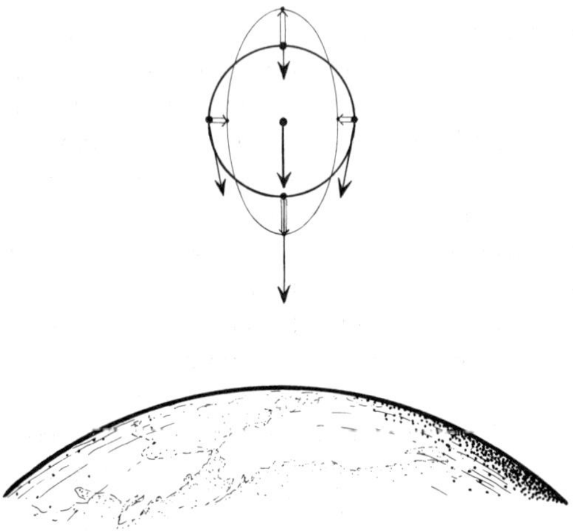

Fig. 6 The effect of Weyl space–time curvature (tidal effect). Double arrows show relative acceleration.

it exactly coincides with Minkowski space. The obstruction to our being able to do this is what is known as *space–time curvature*.

How are we to understand this 'space–time curvature'? In ordinary physical terms, space–time curvature manifests itself in the *tidal* effect of gravity. Imagine oneself situated in space, in free motion under the earth's gravitational field. Imagine, also, that one is surrounded by a sphere of particles, small compared with the size of the earth, but large enough that the slight differences in the earth's field at different points on the sphere are significant. Take the particles to be initially at rest relative to oneself (though all may share one's orbital motion about the earth). Initially, the sphere will seem to remain stationary, since everything falls together in the earth's field (in accordance with Galileo's principle that 'everything falls with the same speed in a gravitational field'); but as soon as the slight differences in the direction and strength of the earth's field on the various particles becomes apparent the sphere will begin to distort into an ellipsoid, stretched in the vertical direction (see Fig. 6). (This is precisely the same effect that the moon's gravitational field has, in raising tides on the earth—where now 'oneself' in the above descriptions is replaced by the earth and the earth by the moon.) In space–time terms, the situation is as depicted in Fig. 7. Notice that the world-lines of the surrounding particles appear to bend towards, and also away from, the central world-line (which represents 'oneself').

The situation is closely analogous to what happens with geodesics drawn on a curved surface. A geodesic is a curve of locally minimum length constrained to the surface. (Imagine a string stretched over the surface.) On a surface of positive curvature (like the surface of a sphere or ellipsoid) close pairs of geodesics that start out parallel will begin to bend inwards towards each other, whereas on a surface of negative curvature (like a saddle surface), they will begin to bend outwards away from each other (see Fig. 8). In our space–time picture of Fig. 7 we have something very similar but where effects of positive and negative curvature are both present at the same time (which can occur here because of the higher dimensionality). In fact the world-lines of particles

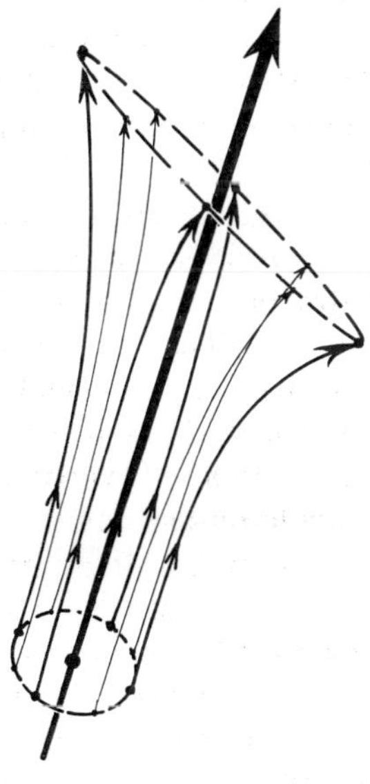

Fig. 7 Space–time curvature: the tidal effect depicted in space–time.

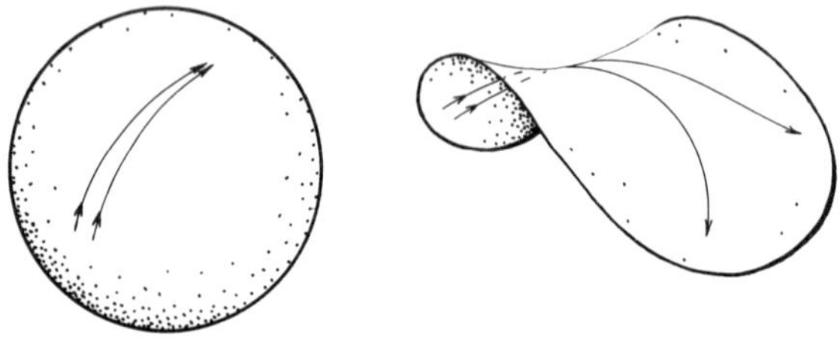

Fig. 8 Geodesics on a curved surface. With positive curvature the goedesics converge, whereas with negative curvature they diverge.

freely moving under gravity *are* geodesics in space–time, where the 'length' involved is the Minkowskian type of length that measures the *time* experienced by a particle—generalized, now, from the flat Minkowskian expression of special relativity in the same way that the length measure along the curved surfaces of Fig. 8 generalizes the length measure in a Euclidean plane. (This Minkowskian time measure is referred to as the 'space–time metric'.) Because of the sign difference in passing from a Euclidean to a Minkowskian type of length, however, it turns out that, in space–time, the world-lines of particles that are freely moving under gravity are geodesics in the sense that they locally *maximize* rather than minimize the time experienced by the particle.

The situation depicted in Fig. 6, which occurs in a region of vacuum, has a very special property: the *volume* of the ellipsoid into which the sphere of particles initially distorts is unchanged from that of the sphere. (This assumes that the sphere is small and that the particles start off at rest relative to one another.) Had the sphere surrounded matter, rather than empty space, then there would have been a volume reduction which, according to *Einstein's field equations*, would have been proportional to the total mass enclosed by the sphere (with a slight correction due to pressures). We can see an example of this by taking our sphere to surround the whole earth rather than being situated in empty space (Fig. 9). Now, there is an acceleration inwards all around the

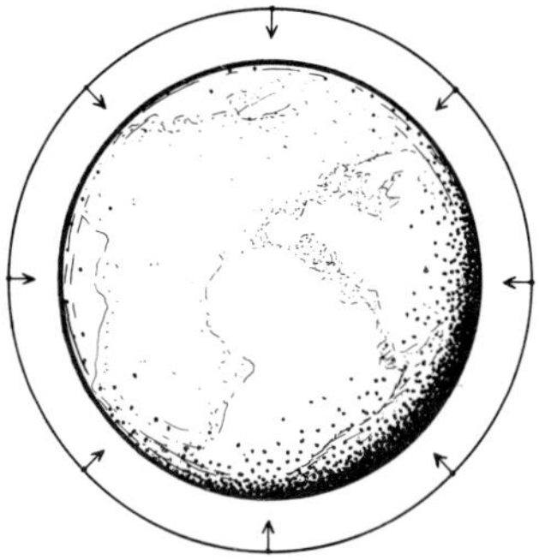

Fig. 9 When the sphere surrounds matter (here the earth), there is a net inwards acceleration. This illustrates the effects of Ricci curvature.

sphere (the normal gravitational acceleration that we experience at the earth's surface), and the volume of the sphere would indeed be reduced. The type of space–time curvature that causes volume reduction is called *Ricci* curvature. Einstein's field equations describe how the Ricci curvature is determined by the energy and momentum densities of matter (and electromagnetic field). There are ten independent components of Ricci curvature, whereas there are twenty components of space–time curvature altogether (the full *Riemann* curvature). The remaining ten components can be collected together into a quantity called the *Weyl* curvature. It is Weyl curvature that describes the distortion, depicted in Fig. 6, due to vacuum space–time curvature. We can think of the Weyl curvature as describing free gravitational field.

The accuracy of Einstein's general relativity is extraordinary. Not only does it inherit all the already remarkable accuracy of Newton's gravitational theory, together with that of Minkowski's space–time (in the absence of gravity), but it achieves much more. It explains the puzzling perihelion advance of Mercury's motion and accurately measured clock-slowing and light-bending effects in gravitational fields. Most impressively of all, it accurately accounts for a slow spiralling inwards of a certain pair of neutron stars in orbit about one another (the binary pulsar PSR 1913+ 16) as an effect due to energy-loss by gravitational waves (a gravitational analogue of Maxwell's electromagnetic waves)—so accurately, in fact, that general relativity can now be regarded as confirmed to an accuracy of about one part in 10^{13}, which makes it, in this sense, the most accurate theory known to science! General relativity is unquestionably a SUPERB theory.

THERMODYNAMICS

The theories that I have been considering up to this point have been concerned with individual bodies and with the nature of the space (–time) in which they move. One might imagine that when large collections of such bodies are considered together, there will be nothing new in principle: it is just a matter of applying the same laws that control individual bodies, albeit in very complicated combinations. Let us restrict attention, for the moment, to Newtonian mechanics. For individual particles, their initial positions and velocities will fix their future motion; the same is true for large collections of particles, and indeed there is a clear sense in which there is nothing in principle that is new when there are very many particles involved.

Of course, with large numbers of bodies, the exact calculations could get prohibitively complicated, but one would expect that approximate procedures could be developed in order to provide an overall picture of what the implications of the dynamical laws would be, even though it would not be possible to keep track of individual particles. The initial positions and velocities of such particles would, in any case, not normally be known in practice, and only a comparatively small number of averaged overall parameters (such as temperature or pressure, for example) might be accessible to observation. Thus, such approximate mathematical procedures would be very valuable—indeed, essential—for the implications of the dynamical laws as applied to individual particles to be understood at the macroscopic level of everyday experience.

But is there anything *physically* new that is needed here; or is it just a matter of mathematical technique? I should make it clear that there has indeed been a vast amount of very valuable mathematical technique (a subject referred to as statistical mechanics) that has been developed to handle such matters, but what is not so readily appreciated is that there *is* actually a new *physical* principle that has crept in, almost unnoticed, under the guise of the *second law of thermodynamics*. This law asserts that the *entropy* of a closed system increases with time (or perhaps remains a constant —in the case of a reversible system). Incidentally, the *first* law of thermodynamics is a statement that the total energy of a closed system remains constant, where the energy content of heat is taken into account. (The subject of thermodynamics arose, mainly in the nineteenth century, from the work of Carnot, Maxwell, Kelvin, Boltzmann, and others, and it developed, in this century, via the work of Gibbs and Einstein, into the subject of statistical mechanics.)

What is entropy? It is best understood in terms of the concept of *phase space*. Phase space is a mathematical space, normally of very large dimension, each of whose points represents the entire state of a physical system at one time, the coordinates of the phase-space point encoding the positions and momenta of all of the various particles that constitute the system (Fig. 10). The dynamical evolution of a system is then described as just the motion of a single phase-space point. To define the (Boltzmann) entropy of a system, we must perform what is called a *coarse-graining* of the phase space (Fig. 11), which means dividing it up into large compartments, where the points in any one compartment are to be taken as representing states that are *indistinguishable* from one another as regards their macroscopic properties. The entropy of a system is then the *logarithm* of the phase-space *volume* (taken in appropriate units) of the compartment to which the point representing that system belongs.

To understand the rough meaning of the second law, think of a system that starts off in some particular configuration of reasonably small entropy and then proceeds in such a way that its entropy increases. For example, consider a glass of water perched on the edge of a table (see Fig. 12). If the glass is nudged, then it is likely to fall to the floor, shattering and spilling its contents irretrievably. In terms of the ordinary Newtonian dynamics of the constituent particles, everything is reversible, and

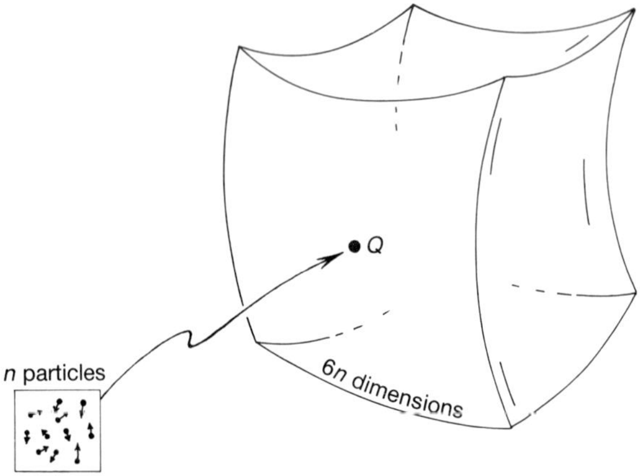

Fig. 10 Phase space: a single point Q of phase space represents the entire state of some physical system, including the instantaneous motions of all its parts.

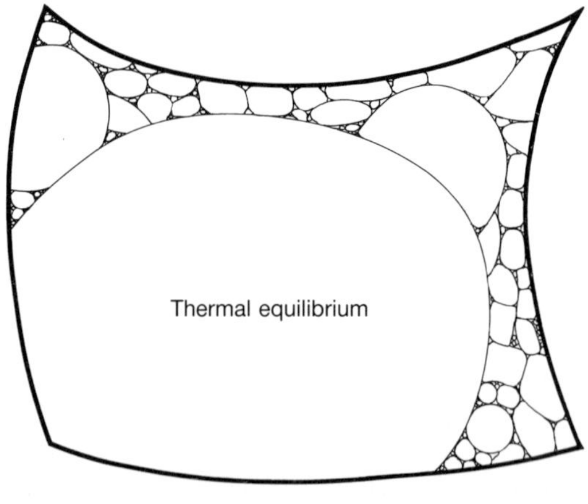

Fig. 11 A coarse-graining of phase space into regions corresponding to states that are macroscopically indistinguishable from one another. The *entropy* is proportional to the logarithm of the phase-space volume.

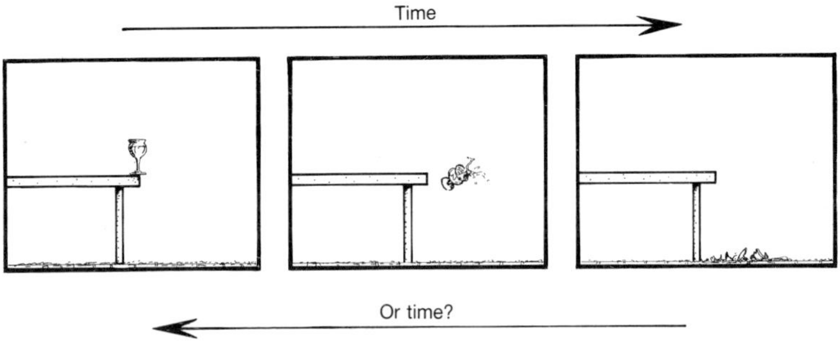

Fig. 12 The laws of mechanics are time reversible; yet the time-ordering of such a scene from the right frame to the left is something that is never experienced, whereas that from the left frame to the right would be commonplace.

there would be nothing against the whole process occurring, instead, in the reverse temporal direction, with little specks of water scattered about the floor collecting together into a glass, which simultaneously assembles itself from innumerable fragments, jumping delicately up in order to balance itself just on the edge of the table. The first progression, however, would be commonplace whilst the second would never occur in practice. What distinguishes the two, from the point of view of thermodynamics, is that the first is in accordance with the second law, whereas the second grossly violates it. The shattered glass and dispersed water droplets provide a state of considerably higher entropy than does that of the glass of water perched on the table. A shattering glass represents an increase in entropy, whereas a self-assembling one would represent a decrease in entropy.

In phase-space terms, we can understand the second law in the following way. Our phase-space point starts in a relatively tiny compartment, but as the point moves, it tends to enter larger and larger compartments as time progresses, see Fig. 13. This is natural, for the larger compartments are liable to have volumes that are utterly enormous compared with the smaller ones, so that once the point has entered a larger one there will, in effect, be no chance that it will find the smaller one again. Explained in this

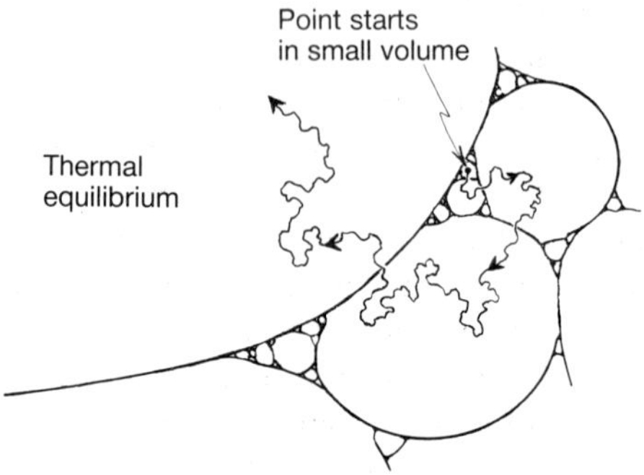

Fig. 13 The second law of thermodynamics in action: as time evolves, the phase-space point enters compartments of larger and larger volume. Consequently the entropy continually increases.

way, the second law seems almost obvious, and it is hard to see why there should be any new physical principle involved here.

However, this 'obviousness' is somewhat deceptive. The laws of Newtonian mechanics are symmetrical with respect to a reversal of the direction of time, yet the second law itself is grossly time *a*symmetric. How can we have deduced a time-asymmetrical law simply from time-symmetrical ones? In fact, we have not. We have made the implicit assumption that it is all right to *start* a system off in a state of low entropy, and then deduce its probable future evolution assuming that there are no low-entropy constraints in the future. If we attempted to use a similar method of reasoning for the most probable *past* behaviour for a system, merely being given its present state, then we would get nonsense. (For example, we would deduce that the most likely way for a glass of water to have got to a state in which its sits perched on the edge of a table is that it spontaneously assembled itself from broken pieces and scattered water droplets, and jumped on to the table by itself!) The difference is that, in the universe that we happen to inhabit, there *was* an enormous low-entropy constraint in the past, whereas there do not appear to be any such constraints in the future.

What was it that happened in the past? I do not want to go into the full discussion of this here, but the upshot of it all is that there must, indeed, have been an absolutely stupendous constraint at the very beginning of time—at an event referred to as the *big bang* origin of the universe. According to modern cosmology, the entire universe was created some 10^{10} years ago in a gigantic explosion. There is a very impressive theory, called the standard model of the hot big bang, that belongs to, at least, the USEFUL category of physical theories. It has many different kinds of confirmation, ranging from the large-scale expansion and uniformity of the universe to detailed information about the nature and proportions of different kinds of atomic elements and particles. (I am almost inclined, myself, to place this theory in the SUPERB category, but perhaps one should be more cautious than this. On the other hand, there are variants and extensions of the standard model that have become popular in recent years, such as 'the inflationary scenario'. But these, it seems to me, cannot yet rise above the category TENTATIVE, in view of the lack of any detailed confirmations.)

How does the standard picture of the big bang serve to constrain the initial universe? I should explain that there are really three distinct classes of standard model, depending upon the spatial geometry that results from the big bang. In one of these models the spatial geometry is Euclidean (referred to as the $k = 0$ model), while in the other two it is either Lobachevskian ($k = -1$) or spherical ($k = +1$). The first two of these models ($k = 0$ or -1) continue to expand indefinitely, whereas the third ($k = +1$) finally recollapses to an event known as the *big crunch*. If anything, present observational evidence favours $k = -1$, but there are very considerable uncertainties, and it is possible that k=0 or +1 might eventually turn out to be more appropriate. For convenience, I shall consider only the $k = +1$ case here, for which the arguments are somewhat clearer than in the other two cases. In Fig. 14, I have given space–time pictures of the early universe and of its entire history in the idealized standard $k = +1$ case. I have suppressed two spatial dimensions, so that the entire spatial universe appears as a horizontal circle (really representing a three-dimensional spherical surface—the surface of a sphere in four-dimensions). The model is idealized because I have ignored all irregularities in the space–time geometry that should be present (according to Einstein's field equations) due to irregularities in the actual

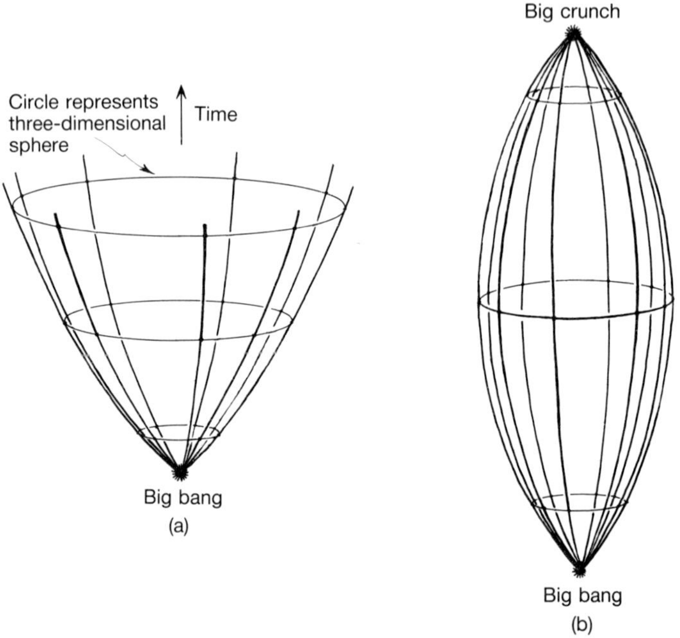

Fig. 14 (a) Space–time picture of an expanding universe with spherical spatial sections (only one space dimension depicted). (b) Eventually this universe recollapses to a final big crunch.

matter distribution. If we include such irregularities, then the picture would be more like that of Fig. 15, in which these irregularities continually increase as time progresses. The final big crunch which can be thought of as the congealing of a large number of black holes) has an immensely more complicated structure than the big bang. This corresponds to the fact that the entropy of the big crunch would be enormously large, whereas that of the big bang was comparatively very tiny, in accordance with the second law. The geometry of the big bang must have been constrained in such a way that corresponds to this low entropy. In effect, this means that the gravitational degrees of freedom that correspond to possible irregularities in the geometry, and which were in principle

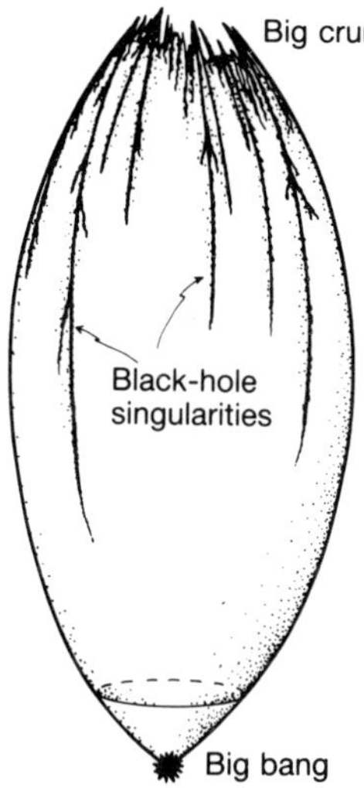

Fig. 15 The entire history of a closed universe starting from a low-entropy big bang, with vanishing Weyl curvature, and ending with a high-entropy big crunch (representing the congealing of many black holes) where the Weyl curvature diverges to infinity.

available to the universe in its early stage, were, for some reason, not actually 'excited' in the big bang as it actually occurred. This remarkable fact has given us the second law of thermodynamics.

I should make it clear to the reader that in the above descriptions I have presented the second law of thermodynamics in a somewhat personal way. Most other physicists would probably not have emphasized cosmology as I have done. Moreover, there are certainly many important aspects of the second law that I have not considered. However, it seems to me that we must turn to cosmology if we are to gain some genuine understanding of a powerful new physical principle, of a time-asymmetrical nature, that must indeed be adjoined to the physical laws that we already understand. Part of this principle must manifest itself in the *boundary condition* for the universe that was the big bang—although there may well be other aspects of such a principle, to do with (as I believe) missing ingredients in relation to quantum theory (and which could conceivably even provide some apparently 'organizational' aspects to structures at a biological or crystallographic level, perhaps in accordance with ideas of some other workers in this field, such as Prigogine).

The big bang is an example of what is called a *space–time singularity*, where the space–time curvature becomes infinite and the equations of general relativity reach their limits of applicability. Other examples of space–time singularities occur in gravitational collapse: in black holes or the big crunch. In order to understand, in physical terms, what is going on in space-time singularities, it will be necessary to obtain a fundamental new physical theory which correctly relates general relatively with quantum theory: *quantum gravity*. Such a theory is at present lacking, but it seems clear to me that one of its features must be a *time asymmetry*, in order that the structure of singularities will differ profoundly depending upon whether they are of *past-type* (the big bang) or of *future-type* (in black holes or the big crunch). The past-type singularities appear to be enormously constrained (low entropy)—apparently in such a way that the Weyl part of the space-time curvature goes to zero (or is at least comparatively small, in relation to the Ricci part), whereas the future-type singularities are not so constrained. The enormity of such a constraint can be seen by an example: if the universe (assuming $k = +1$) contains of the order of 10^{80} particles, then the region of phase space that it would be constrained to at the big bang would be only about one part in $10^{10^{123}}$ of the entire phase-space volume! (This corresponds to an entropy difference of 10^{123}; recall the logarithm in the definition of entropy. The value depends upon an expression for black-hole entropy due to Bekenstein and Hawking.)

When I refer to thermodynamics as a SUPERB theory, I do not mean to be taking figures like those just given as a measure of its accuracy, since in my discussion I have taken things considerably away from what is standard in thermodynamic theory—which does not normally involve considerations of cosmology. Nevertheless, there is indeed something extraordinarily precise about the second law. This is despite the impression of imprecision involved in the concept of entropy, an impression that is in many respects justified in view of the arbitrariness in the concept of coarse-graining, etc. For reasons such as this, I had initially felt reluctant to place thermodynamics in the SUPERB category—or, indeed, to think of it as a physical theory at all in the sense of the others. On reflection, however, I have come to the conclusion that its characterization as a SUPERB physical theory is amply justified, in view of the extraordinary degree of organization that it implies for the structure of the universe in the past.

QUANTUM MECHANICS

The most enigmatic of the SUPERB theories is undoubtedly quantum mechanics, which arose in the first quarter of this century from the combined efforts of many outstanding scientists: particularly Planck, Einstein, Bohr, Heisenberg, Schrödinger, de Broglie, Born, Jordan, Pauli, and Dirac. If we take into account the breadth of applicability of this theory and its far-reaching nature, then is it also the most accurate of the SUPERB theories (where I mean this accuracy to be taken in a different sense from the precision exhibited in a single phenomenon, in the case of general relativity, or the somewhat obscure sense of the precision involved in thermodynamics) The enigmatic nature of this theory lies in the combination of this extraordinary precision when the theory is applied to phenomena that, in a certain sense, are on a 'small scale'—I shall call this scale the *quantum level*—and a bewildering absurdity if one tires to apply the theory in the same way at the macroscopic level of everyday experience—called the *classical level*. Almost as bewildering is the multitude of different attitudes that are adopted by physicists and philosophers in order to come to terms with, or perhaps explain away, the apparent (or real?) absurdities. It is inevitable that, in a short account like this, I shall display a considerable personal bias. I make no apology for this, but the reader is hereby warned that not everyone views the subject quite as I do. What is *not* controversial, however, is the *mathematical* formalism of the theory, and how this formalism is applied in practice, so let me start by giving a very brief account of what we shall need of this.

There is a very basic principle in quantum mechanics known as the *superposition principle*, which asserts that if two alternative things $\mathbb{A}$ and $\mathbb{B}$ might happen, then weighted combinations $w\mathbb{A}+z\mathbb{B}$ can also happen. What does that mean? It may be vaguely helpful if just for the moment we try to think of w and z as *probabilities*. Then $w\mathbb{A}+z\mathbb{B}$ would be interpreted as some kind of probability-weighted assertion that either $\mathbb{A}$ or $\mathbb{B}$ might be happening, but we do not know which, and the relative probability of $\mathbb{A}$ to $\mathbb{B}$ is the ratio of the numbers w to z. This might have been fine had w and z been ordinary positive real numbers, but—and this is the shock—w and z are *complex* numbers!

I should remind the reader what a complex number is. It is a number constructed from ordinary real numbers and the *square root of minus one*. More precisely, it is a number that can be written as $x+\mathrm{i}y$, where x and y are real numbers and where $\mathrm{i}^2=-1$. This may seem very mysterious, but for the moment, just think of this as a bit of mathematics. I shall try to illucidate the physical meaning of all this in a moment. As mathematical objects, complex numbers make perfectly good sense. You can add them or multiply them out: if $w = u + \mathrm{i}v$ and $z = x + \mathrm{i}y$, then $w + z = (u + x) + \mathrm{i}(v + y)$ and $wz = (ux - vy) + \mathrm{i}(vx + uy)$, where u, v, x, and y are real. It is also very helpful to use a geometrical representation of complex numbers as points in a Euclidean plane (often referred to as the *Argand plane*; see Fig. 16), where the complex

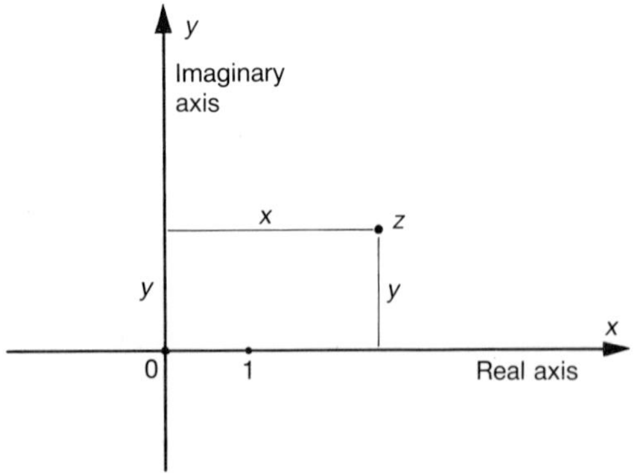

Fig. 16 The Argand plane, depicting a complex number $z = x + \mathrm{i}y$.

number $z = x + iy$ is represented as the point with Cartesian coordinates (x,y). The rules for adding and multiplying complex numbers have simple geometrical interpretations in terms of the Argand plane.

Let us now return to quantum mechanics? How are we to interpret the superposition $w\mathbb{A} + z\mathbb{B}$? It is certainly *not* a probability-weighted pair of alternatives after all, since a probability cannot be a general complex number. Instead, we must think of it as just another physical alternative, different from either $\mathbb{A}$ or $\mathbb{B}$. At least this is how things seem to behave at the quantum level. As soon as the effects of $\mathbb{A}$ and of $\mathbb{B}$ can independently get magnified to the classical level, then we do *not* allow the possibility of $w\mathbb{A} + z\mathbb{B}$, but we find that *either* $\mathbb{A}$ *or* $\mathbb{B}$ occurs with indeed a probability weighting, but the relative probabilities of $\mathbb{A}$ and $\mathbb{B}$ are not w and z, but their *squared moduli* $|w|^2$ and $|z|^2$. (The squared modulus of a complex number z is the square of the distance that the point representing it in the Argand plane lies from the origin, i.e. it is $|z|^2 = x^2 + y^2$, where $z = x + iy$, with x and y real.)

The procedure whereby the quantum state $w\mathbb{A} + z\mathbb{B}$ appears suddenly to get converted into either the state $\mathbb{A}$ or the state $\mathbb{B}$, with relative probability weightings $|w|^2$ and $|z|^2$, whenever the effects of $\mathbb{A}$ and $\mathbb{B}$ get amplified to the classical level, is called *reduction of the state vector* (or collapse of the wavefunction), and I denote it by the letter **R**. (Strictly speaking, this happens only for states $\mathbb{A}$ and $\mathbb{B}$ that are what are called *orthogonal*, but I shall not try to define precisely what this means. Think of $\mathbb{A}$ and $\mathbb{B}$ simply as being appropriately *independent* of one another.) For a system that remains entirely at the quantum level, however, the process **R** seems never to occur. Instead, there is a *deterministic* procedure, that I denote by the letter **U**, giving the evolution of the quantum state, called *unitary evolution*, which is governed by a precise (partial) differential equation called the *Schrödinger equation*. The procedure **U** differs from **R** in almost every conceivable respect: **U** is continuous, deterministic, local (in configuration space), and time-symmetric, whereas **R** is discontinuous, non-deterministic, non-local, and time-asymmetric. Moreover, **U** is *linear*, in the sense that the **U**-evolution of the state $w\mathbb{A} + z\mathbb{B}$ is precisely the same as the complex-weighted superposition of the independent

U-evolutions of the state A and the state B separately, where the complex weighting factors w and z remain *constant*. This is certainly not true for **R**.

Many physicists are of the opinion that the process **R** should not be considered as a real physical process, but it arises as some kind of 'illusion' or approximation, when a system becomes large or complicated, or when it becomes inextricably interconnected with the physical environment. For my own part, I cannot see how this alone could be the case. The procedures **U** and **R** are just too mathematically different from one another; in particular, I cannot see how two superposed states can ever get themselves *un*superposed, merely by evolving according to the procedure **U**, nor do I see how the time-asymmetry inherent in **R** can arise merely through the action of **U**. Other physicists (or, quite often, the same physicists as before) try to take the line that it is **U** that is the illusion, and there is actually no 'reality' at all at the quantum level. Instead, they may claim to be driven to an entirely 'subjective' view of the quantum world (although this is not the usual sense of the word 'subjective', as far as I can make out) and often they would simply regard the mathematical formalism as being merely a convenient procedure for calculating various probabilities for the different results of 'measurements' that might be performed on a system. I have great difficulties with such viewpoints also, since I do not see how we can dispense with physical reality, even at the quantum level. Moreover, the mathematical procedures for describing the quantum level are so precise and accurate that I do not see how they can fail to be reflecting some kind of precise reality that is indeed taking place at the level of quantum phenomena.

In order to clarify the mathematical procedures, it will be helpful to take a look at a simple example of a quantum system. Let us consider a single particle of 'spin one-half', say an electron or proton. Its state of spin can be characterized by a direction in space about which it may be spinning in a right-handed or left-handed sense. The usual convention is to take the right-handed sense as counting as positive and the left-handed one as negative, so we take the left-handed particle as spinning (positively) about the *opposite* direction in space. Now, for a spin-one-half particle we can take all the states of spin to be superpositions of (states of

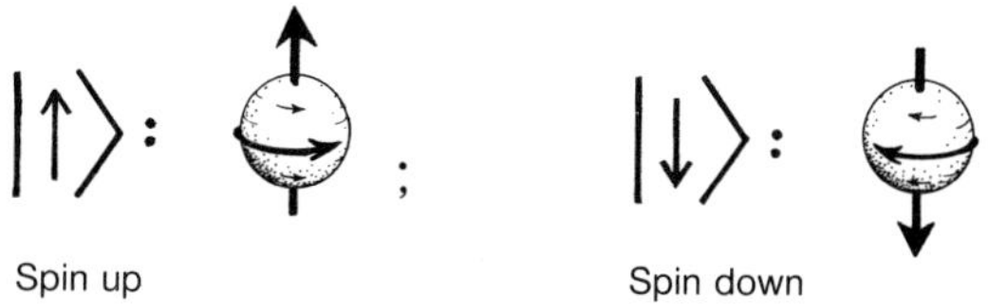

Fig. 17 Two independent (orthogonal) states for the spin states of a spin one-half particle, e.g. an electron, are *spin up* (right-handed about the upward vertical) and *spin down* (right-handed about the downward vertical). All other spin stages are expressible as combinations of these.

spin about) just two opposite directions, say up, written $|\uparrow\rangle$, and down, written $|\downarrow\rangle$ (see Fig. 17.) The general state of spin, say $|\nearrow\rangle$, will be some superposition of these two states: $|\nearrow\rangle = w|\uparrow\rangle + z|\downarrow\rangle$. There is nothing special about the directions 'up' and 'down', so there is nothing special about our original states $|\uparrow\rangle$ and $|\downarrow\rangle$ (except that they must be orthogonal to each other, which in this situation means *opposite* directions in space). We could equally have chosen any other pair of opposite directions to start with, say 'right' $|\rightarrow\rangle$ and 'left' $|\leftarrow\rangle$, and then expressed the general state of spin (and, in particular, 'up' or 'down') in terms of these other two. This illustrates the fact that, at the quantum level, superposed states are no less (and no more) real than the original states that they are superpositions of. Another point is also illustrated. This is that the complex numbers that appear in these superpositions, though mysterious in their interpretations in relation to probability, make good *geometrical* sense. The geometrical space of possible ratios $w{:}z$ of pairs of complex numbers w and z is a *sphere* (referred to as the *Riemann* sphere), and this sphere can be directly related to the Argand plane that we considered earlier (see Fig. 18). Here, the complex number $q=z/w$ corresponds to a point on the Argand plane (or to infinity, if $w=0$), and we can refer this to the sphere by projection from the south pole (a correspondence referred to as *stereographic* projection). The point that q corresponds to on the sphere gives the direction of spin for the quantum state $|\nearrow\rangle = w|\uparrow\rangle + z|\downarrow\rangle$

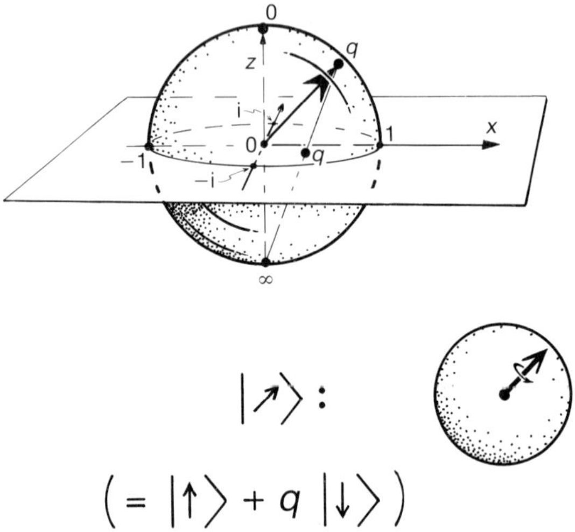

Fig. 18 The Riemann sphere, here represented as the space of physically distinct spin states of a spin one-half particle. The sphere is projected stereographically from its south pole (∞) to the Argand plane through its equator.

(which is physically the same as $w^{-1}|\nearrow\rangle = |\uparrow\rangle + q|\downarrow\rangle$, since only the *ratios* of the coefficients w and z are regarded as physically significant, according to the theory).

If we now wish to 'make a measurement' of the spin, we select a direction in space and orient our measuring apparatus in that direction. Let $\mathbb{A}$ represent the state of spin in that direction and $\mathbb{B}$, the state of spin in the diametrically opposite direction. The apparatus serves to amplify the effects of $\mathbb{A}$ and $\mathbb{B}$ to the classical level, so we must now regard all possible states of spin as superpositions of *these* two, whatever the original state of spin might have been. The result of our measurement must be either $\mathbb{A}$ or $\mathbb{B}$, with respective probabilities in fact given by $\cos^2\theta$ and $\sin^2\theta$, where the original state of spin of our particle was tilted at an angle θ to the chosen direction. The state of spin must now 'jump' to either $\mathbb{A}$ or $\mathbb{B}$, with these respective probabilities, in accordance with the procedure **R**, whereas if we had chosen *not* to make a measurement, the state of spin could have been kept at the quantum level, and it would then have evolved, perhaps precessing in some way, or remaining constant, according to the procedure **U**, and this evolution could be checked by performing some other measurement at some later time.

An important feature of quantum mechanics is the way that systems involving several particles must be treated. For example, for a system consisting of just two particles, say an electron and a proton, the state $\mathbb{A}$ might describe the electron as being at some particular point E and the proton, at some point P, while the state $\mathbb{B}$ might describe the electron as being at F and the proton at Q. The superposition principle asserts that $\mathbb{A} + \mathbb{B}$ is also a possible state. This is an example of what is called an *entangled* (or correlated) state, and it exhibits a peculiar property characteristic of such states. Suppose that we decide to measure the position of the electron (i.e. we set up some experimental situation in which the respective effects of the electron being at E or F are magnified to macroscopically distinguishable outcomes). Then we find that the whole state must jump to $\mathbb{A}$ if the electron is found to be at E and to $\mathbb{B}$ if the electron is found to be at F. The remarkable thing about such a measurement of an entangled state is that the measurement of the *electron* seems to cause the *proton's* state to jump simultaneously with it: in the first case, the proton ending up at the point P and in the second, at Q. This would be the case no matter how distant the proton might be from the electron. There would appear to be some mysterious action of the measurement on the proton, even though it is only the electron that is being measured. This action seems to have to occur *instantaneously* even though the proton could be many metres, or perhaps light-years away from the measuring apparatus. This is what Einstein, in expressing his deep unease with the physical implications of quantum theory, referred to as 'spooky action at a distance'. On the face of it there would appear to be a contradiction with the principles of Einstein's relativity, since the very concept of what 'instantaneous' means is dependent upon the motion of the 'observer' in whose reference frame the physical description is being made. In fact there is no conflict with the *observational* aspects of relativity; in particular it is not possible to send a message faster than light using this 'spooky action', although there is a distinct conflict with the *spirit* and with the space–time descriptions of relativity theory. There are serious problems that are still not completely resolved in making the principles of special relativity and quantum mechanics consistent with one another. (We shall be touching on a little of this in the next section.) The problem of combining the principles of *general* relativity and quantum mechanics is considerably more serious, and remains one of the deep stumbling blocks to fundamental progress in theoretical physics.

I should clarify one point about Einstein's 'spooky action'. One can envisage an apparently similar situation that can occur with ordinary classical bodies. Imagine a box which is known to contain one white ball and one black ball. Suppose that the balls are taken out and removed to two opposite corners of the room, without either being looked at. If one ball is examined and found to be white (like the electron, above, being found to be at the point E) then the other ball must be black (like the proton being consequently at P). If, on the other hand, the first ball is found to be in the state 'black' (like the electron found at F), then the second ball's uncertain state appears to jump instantaneously to 'white' (proton found at Q). But no one would attribute the sudden change of the second ball's 'uncertain' state to being 'black with certainty' or to being 'white with certainty', to some mysterious non-local 'spooky action' travelling to it instantaneously from the first ball the moment that first ball is examined. The point is, however, that the quantum-mechanical situation often can*not* be treated in the same way as the balls just considered, where in that case there was an underlying 'reality' about where the white and black balls actually were. In quantum mechanics, one has to treat an entangled state as a single entity and not as a pair of subsystems that behave independently of one another (like the black and white balls) when they are widely enough separated from one another.

An example (suggested by Bohm, illustrating earlier ideas due to Einstein, Rosen, and Podolsky—and often referred to as the 'EPR paradox') is an entangled system consisting of two spin one-half particles (say an electron and a proton) that are known to start in a state for which the total spin is zero. When they are separated, the spin of the electron must be opposite to that of the proton, though the spin direction of either may not be defined on its own. If some direction in space is selected, and the electron's state of spin is measured in that direction, then it must (instantaneously) turn out that the state of spin of the proton is in the opposite direction. If one could measure the actual direction of the proton's state of spin then it would be possible to use the orientation of the electron-measuring apparatus as a signalling device that could transmit messages faster than light (since the proton's spin-axis is apparently instantaneously fixed to be in the selected direction). However, all that the rules of quantum mechanics allow is that that probability values are given to the two possible spin values (i.e. right-handed or left-handed) about a *chosen* direction for the measurement of the proton's spin. It turns out that these probabilities are such that (a) no signal can indeed be sent in this way, and (b) *no* description can in fact be given where the electron and proton are considered as independent physical objects (like the black and white balls considered above)—as follows from a famous theorem due to Bell. Certain careful and ingenious experiments of this general nature have been carried out over the past twenty years, and have demonstrated, via Bell's theorem, the inadequacy of a 'local' description of physical reality, in which the electron and photon in the above description could be considered as independent objects. The most impressive of these experiments was performed by Aspect and his co-workers in Paris in the early 1980s. The experiment used photons, rather than the electron–proton pair of my description above, but the principle is the same.

There are many other respects in which quantum mechanics remains an enigmatic and baffling theory. Most of these have to do with the **U-R** conflict referred to above, and it is fair to say that there are fundamental aspects of the interpretation (at least) of the theory that are unresolved. It seems that we must use one deterministic theory at the quantum level of phenomena—where **U** holds strong—and another quite different deterministic theory (classical physics) at the classical level. When effects are magnified from the quantum to the classical level, we must bring in the *in*deterministic procedure **R**. There are some physicists (probably only a small minority) who believe that **U** holds at all levels, but that when a 'measurement' takes place the observer's conscious state becomes entangled with the result of that measurement, so that his being consciously aware of one outcome of an experiment is entangled with that particular outcome, while his awareness of another outcome is entangled with that other outcome; yet both states of awareness and both outcomes must coexist in the 'actual' state of the universe. This is the so-called 'many-worlds' view (although a much larger number of 'pragmatic' physicists would claim to be able to follow this route without reaching its 'many-worlds' logical conclusion). Another (probably also unpopular) view is that the rules of quantum theory must be changed whenever consciousness enters the picture. My own view (no doubt also unpopular) is that the rules of quantum theory must indeed be changed at some level, but this change will arise because of the effects of quantum gravity (which implies that, roughly speaking, the process **R** comes in when the superposed states of a quantum system get entangled with as much mass as the so-called Planck mass, which is abut 10^{-5} grams) and that it is in relation to the time assymetry that must be present in quantum gravity that the time-asymmetric aspects of the **R** procedure will eventually be understood. In any case, even the standard theory is unclear about what it is that actually constitutes a 'measurement', so that, for whatever reason, the process **R** comes into play. Problems remain, no matter what viewpoint one adopts.

Be that as it may, quantum mechanics is undoubtedly a SUPERB theory. Its applicability to physical behaviour at the quantum level remains supreme, and no phenomena are known that contradict the theory. Moreover, it explains many things, both familiar and novel that seem incomprehensible on the basis of classical ideas (such as spectral lines, chemical bonding, the colours of heated substance, solidity, freezing and boiling, the accuracy of heredity, lasers, superconductivity, superfluidity, etc.) always with complete agreement between theory and observation—to the extent that the theory can, at present, be actually worked out.

QUANTUM ELECTRODYNAMICS

The subject of *quantum field theory* is the application of the procedures of quantum mechanics to a (relativistic) classical field theory—such as Maxwell's electrodynamics. We say that it is the theory obtained by *quantizing* that field theory. Alternatively, we may view quantum field theory as the subject that has arisen from attempts to make quantum theory consistent with special relativity. In the context of quantum theory, 'fields' and 'systems of identical particles' turn out to be the same thing, so that quantizing Maxwell's field, for example, is the same as quantizing a system of relativistic particles of the appropriate kind—in this case 'photons', which are massless particles of unit spin. I have chosen to separate quantum field theory from ordinary (non-relativistic) quantum theory, as described in the previous section, because quantum field theory brings in a number of new ingredients, and these can give rise to some very serious problems. The nature of these new problems is that if one strictly applies the quantum-mechanical rules to an interacting relativistic field, then one simply gets the answer 'infinity', rather than something sensible. In a general way, this comes about because a field theory involves an infinite number of degrees of freedom, so the quantum superpositions that have to be considered in a process are much more extensive than they are in a theory with a finite number of particles. These infinities have to be eliminated from the theory before it can be used. This turns out to be possible for certain types of quantum field theories—called *renormalizable theories*—but the procedures are somewhat artificial, going strictly outside what quantum theory tells us to do, and they involve the loss of certain kinds of information from the theory. For this reason, quantum field theory is, strictly speaking, a different theory from ordinary quantum theory, and its status as a SUPERB theory, or otherwise, must be considered separately.

The most successful of the quantum field theories is undoubtedly *quantum electrodynamics* (or QED) which involves not only the quantized electromagnetic field—i.e. *photons*—but also *electrons*, using Dirac's famous equation for the electron that he introduced in 1931. QED emerged from work of Jordan, Heisenberg, and Pauli in the mid-1920s; it was formulated by Dirac in 1926–34, but had to wait until 1947–9 to be made workable by the elimination of infinities, according to the process of *renormalization*, as was done by Bethe, Schwinger, Feynman, and Tomonaga. Feynman also introduced a number of conceptual and technical innovations that have been very influential. One of these was the *path integral* (based partly on an earlier idea due to Dirac) according to which all possible space–time *histories* must be superposed—including histories in which particles are allowed to wander backwards and forwards in time as well as space (see Fig. 19). The interpretation of an electron, when it wanders backwards in time, is that then it is a *positron*—i.e. an *anti*-electron. As the electron's space–time path bends around from being future-pointing to past-pointing, this is interpreted as the annihilation of the electron by a positron; and when the path bends back again from being past-pointing to future-pointing, there is creation of a new electron, in association with this positron.

In fact, the physical existance of positrons was a prediction of Dirac's original theory of electrons, and it was soon confirmed in observation (by Anderson in 1932). Moreover, it is a general consequence of the principles of quantum field theory that *every* particle must have its corresponding *antiparticle* (sometimes, as in the case of a photon, a particle of the same kind as the original one). Any massive particle can annihilate its antiparticle to form energy, and such a pair can be created out of energy. It is a

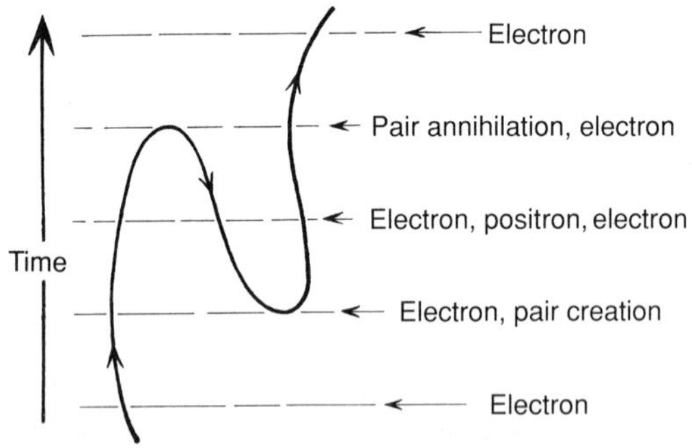

Fig. 19 In a Feynman path integral, all possible classical histories, for the type of particle in question (here an electron), must be superposed. The classical history can involve the particle travelling 'backwards in time' which is interpreted as the particle's antiparticle (here a positron) travelling forwards in time. One such contribution to the path integral is depicted here.

characteristic feature of quantum field theory that the number of particles of each different kind, in a physical system, need not be a constant; nor need this number even be definite, since superpositions of states with different numbers of particles and antiparticles are allowed.

Another influential (and related) innovation due to Feynman (and Dyson) was what are now called *Feynman diagrams*. These are graphical representations of certain mathematical expressions (integrals—which, when taken at face value, are unfortunately usually infinite) that can be used to calculate virtually anything that is needed in quantum field theory. What makes Feynman diagrams conceptually very convenient is that they give us pictures of the various physical processes that can contribute, in superposition, to the total effect. In Fig. 20, I have drawn some of the Feynman diagrams for a situation in which an electron and a positron annihilate to produce two photons. The diagrams shown

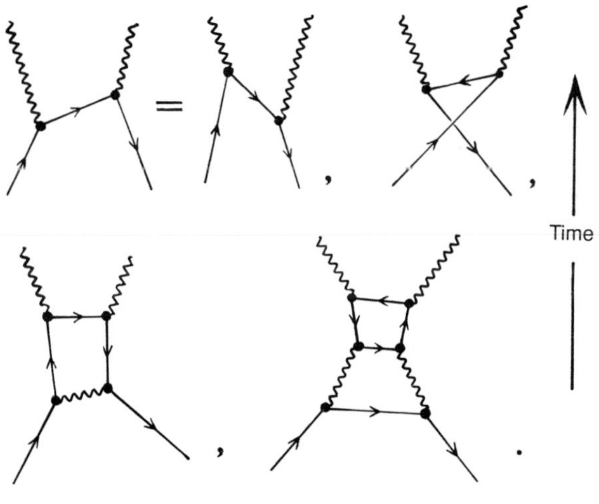

Fig. 20 Various Feynman diagrams are depicted, representing processes that contribute, in superposition, to the total effect when an electron and a positron annihilate to produce two photons. (Electrons and positrons are represented as straight lines with arrows; photons are represented as wavy lines.)

are all concerned with QED, where only electrons, positrons, and photons are involved. Other quantum field theories would involve further particles, such as mesons, or quarks, gluons, etc.

QED exhibits an extraordinary precision, in the comparatively small number of situations for which the theory can be worked through and compared with accurate experiment. In particular, the value of the magnetic moment of an electron is calculated to be 1.00115965246 (in appropriate units, with an allowance for an error of about 20 in the last two digits). This may be compared with a recent experimental value, which is 1.00115965221 (with a possible error of about 4 in the last digit). (Electrons behave like tiny magnets of spinning electric charge, and the term 'magnetic moment' refers to the strength of this tiny magnet.) As Feynman has pointed out, this kind of accuracy could determine the distance between New York and Los Angeles to within the width of a human hair. There are a few other results, of comparable accuracy. Quantum electrodynamics is indeed a SUPERB theory.

THE USEFUL QUANTUM FIELD THEORIES

No quantum field theory other than QED can match this kind of accuracy. However there are two quantum field theories that , it seems to me, come clearly into the USEFUL category. The first of these is called *electroweak* theory, and the second is referred to as *quantum chromodynamics*, or QCD. The first, put forward by Salam, Ward, Glashow, and Weinberg, in about 1967, is a theory of the *weak* interactions that are responsible for radioactive decay, combining them, in an appropriate way, with QED. The second, QCD, is a theory of the *strong* interactions that bind protons and neutrons together to form atomic nuclei; it is also a theory of the very structure of the strongly interacting particles themselves (protons, neutrons, mesons, etc.). These particles are regarded as being built up, according to a scheme due to Gell Mann and Zweig, from more elementary ingredients, called *quarks* (and gluons), although these ingredients are never seen on their own. Both electroweak theory and QCD are what are called *gauge theories*, and are based on a generalization of Maxwell's electrodynamics called *Yang–Mills* theory that was introduced by Yang and Mills in 1954, although, unknown to them, the theory had also been studied a good deal earlier by Pauli (and by Shaw). In order to be applicable to the (strong or weak) interactions of actual physical massive particles, Yang–Mills theory has to be modified from the original version of the theory (where, like the photon, the mediating particles need to be massless). The necessary modifications arose out of a prescription due to Higgs (and Kibble). An ingredient that is incorporated into electroweak theory is the parity-violating effect (mirror-reflection asymmetry) that was observed in weak interactions (beta-decay) by Wu and her collaborators after having been predicted by Yang and Lee. According to the theory of QCD, there is an (unobservable) quantum property referred to as 'colour' (nothing to do with ordinary colours), from which QCD gets its name. There are certain interconnections and consistency requirements between electroweak theory and QCD, and the combination of the two theories is sometimes referred to as the *standard model* of particle physics.

Although there are no observed discrepancies with either electroweak theory or QCD, as far as I know, there is nothing like the very precise agreement with experiment that can be seen in the case of QED. It is perhaps fair to say that there is about *one* decimal place of numerical agreement between the predictions of the standard model and observation. It may be that this comparatively poor level of agreement is merely a reflection of the calculational difficulties that are inherent in the theory. On the other hand, it is possible that these calculational difficulties are simply serving to obscure some essential defect that may be present. Also, it must be said that there is a considerable untidiness in the standard model, and there are many apparently arbitrary parameters involved (masses of basic constituent particles, strengths of basic interactions, etc.). It seems clear to me that both electroweak theory and QCD are examples of USEFUL theories, and that more understanding (if not an overhaul of some basic principles) will be needed before a SUPERB theory of fundamentical particles is to emerge.

SOME MODERN TENTATIVE THEORIES

There are many attempts to find such a theory, but none of those can rise above the category TENTATIVE, since none have any significant experimental support (beyond any observational evidence that may have been part of the input into the theory in the first place). Among the most 'conventional' of these TENTATIVE theories are the so-called *grand unified* (or GUT) theories. These attempt to provide the same kind of unification between electroweak theory and QCD that electroweak theory itself achieved between the earlier theories of weak interactions with QED. In all these theories, it is assumed that the various physical interactions concerned are all part of the same scheme, interrelated by a large symmetry group. This symmetry would be exact at extremely high temperatures, but a process of 'symmetry breaking' sets in at lower temperatures which enables the different interactions to be distinguished from one another, and their smaller symmetry groups 'frozen out'. (The Higgs–Kibble procedure mentioned above makes use of this. Moreover, the TENTATIVE *inflation* theory of the early universe that I briefly mentioned in relation to the standard model of the big bang relies critically on this procedure.)

A TENTATIVE idea that was fashionable some ten or so years ago was a development of a much older theory (put forward by Kaluza and Klein in the 1920s) whereby space–time was envisaged as having more than the four dimensions that we are physically aware of, the extra dimensions being 'compactified', which here means that they are, in a sense, curled up into a tight ball of tiny size. The compactified dimensions are supposed to give rise to physical interactions, separate from the interaction of gravitation that arises from the ordinary four space–time dimensions in accordance with Einstein's general relativity. (The original Kaluza–Klein theory was five-dimensional, with one extra dimension to describe electromagnetism.) To get a picture of this kind of thing, imagine the surface of a hosepipe. On a large scale the pipe resembles a *one*-dimensional curve (to be thought of analogous to the four-dimensional space–time), but on closer examination, we find that the hosepipe surface is actually *two*-dimensional, one of the dimensions being compactified in this way. (One of the most popular Kaluza–Klein-type theories was eleven-dimensional, with seven dimensions compactified in the form of a 'squashed 7-sphere'.)

Another (still currently) popular idea is that of *supersymmetry*, according to which each particle of nature is accompanied by a sister particle whose spin differs from its own by half a unit. The idea of supersymmetry is based on the study of certain mathematical kinds of number that are intriguing (and, in some contexts, important) in their own right. When combined with the ideas of general relativity, supersymmetry gives rise to a theory called *supergravity*. One of the initial advantages of supergravity theory over standard general relativity was supposed to have been that it made the resulting quantized gravitational theory renormalizable (when it had not been before). However, these initial optimistic hopes have not been fulfilled and the original supergravity theory has somewhat fallen from favour.

Combining ingredients from all the above TENTATIVE theories is the (still) very fashionable (super)string theory. The basic *new* ingredient is a revival of an ingenious idea that was put forward by Nambu in 1970 in order to explain certain puzzling phenomena of strongly interacting particles. The theory was revived in a different form by Green and Schwarz in 1984, partly with an eye to describing gravitational interactions at the basic level, rather than the strong interactions, so as to provide a quantum gravity theory free of the non-renormalizable infinities that seemed to occur with standard quantization procedures applied to Einstein's theory. There have been strong claims, from time to time that not only does string theory provide a finite theory of quantum gravity, but that it also gives us a 'theory of everything'. Though I have no doubt that such claims are overstated and that the theory is firmly in the category TENTATIVE, having no support whatever on the observational side, it does have some points of considerable interest, and a brief description of the basic ideas is not at all out of place here.

The central idea is that the basic physical entities, or 'particles' in the theory are not the ordinary pointlike particles of conventional theory but extended objects that are to be thought of as little one-dimensional loops (or perhaps little open curves). In space–time terms, these so-called *strings* will describe two-dimensional surfaces, replacing the one-dimensional world-lines of conventional relativity theory. These surfaces are to be treated as the ingredients of a quantum field theory, and in Fig. 21 I have indicated the kind of way in which these surfaces would replace the lines of a standard Feynman diagram. One of the most intriguing features of these string surfaces is that several apparently different processes, that in Feynman diagram terms would have to be treated as different, may turn out to be actually the same from the point of view of string theory. (This was an important property of the original Nambu string theory, which explained certain observational features of strongly interacting particles, although in the modern versions of string theory, this connection with observational matters has become obscured.) An important aspect of string theory is that most of the infinities that arise in conventional quantum field theory now disappear. The frequent over-optimistic claims that string theory provides (in particular) a finite quantum

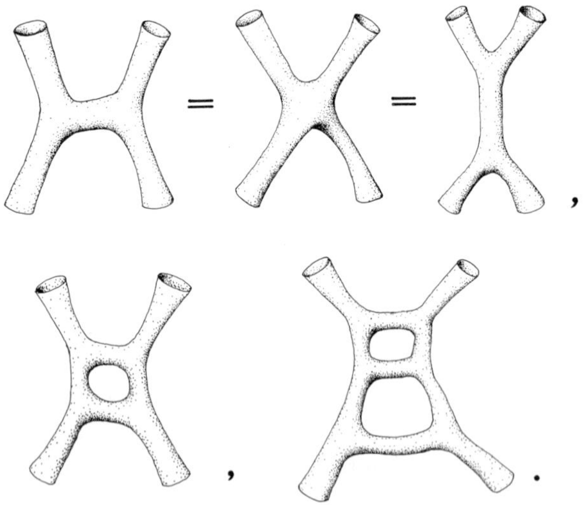

Fig. 21 Various string histories are depicted, the totality of which must occur in superposition. The upper three string histories all represent the same process since they can be deformed into one another.

gravity theory arose from this kind of reason. However, there are still infinities (and also conceptual problems) that arise when one tries to add together the effects due to string surfaces with all different possible topologies (which the theory tells us we are supposed to do). An even more serious conceptual problem is that the theory (at least in most of its original versions) required that the strings propagate through a space–time of twenty-six dimensions, or else of ten dimensions if the appropriate ideas from supersymmetry are also incorporated (to give *super*string theory). In fact, for various other reasons also, (super)string theory is very far indeed from providing an adequate quantum gravity theory, let alone a theory of everything.

On the other hand, there are important *mathematical* reasons why string theory has been taken seriously as a model that could perhaps provide some deep insights into the workings of nature at the sub-particle level. These reasons arise largely from the relation between the string surfaces and complex numbers. Recall the Riemann sphere that I referred to in connection with the spin of an electron, and with the way in which the complex numbers of quantum theory relate to the geometry of directions in physical space. The Riemann sphere is the simplest example of what may be called a *complex curve*, or complex one-dimensional space. In the complex sense, it is *one*-, rather than two-dimensional space because, as in the case of the Argand plane, a *single* complex number takes over the role of a *pair* of real numbers. More complicated complex curves can have more elaborate topological structures, such as that of a torus (surface of a ring) or of a sphere with several 'handles'. Such complex curves are referred to as *Riemann surfaces*. The power of string theory, in mathematical terms, lies in the close connection between string surfaces and these Riemann surfaces.

There is another body of ideas that represents an attempt to relate the theory of complex spaces (but now of higher dimension) to space–time structure and quantum mechanics. This is *twistor* theory, and it is the approach that I have been most involved with myself. Insofar as twistor theory is concerned with providing a new physical picture of nature, it must belong to the category TENTATIVE also. (It certainly provides no new physical predictions that could be put to observational test.) But twistors may also be viewed in a more modest light than this, namely as giving a mere *mathematical* reformulation of *existing* physical theory, particularly in the context of special (or general) relativity. It provides unusual insights into Maxwellian electrodynamics and quantum field theory.

The two most important motivational ideas that are incorporated into twistor theory are, first, a fundamental use of *complex numbers* and complex spaces (as just referred to in connection with string theory) and, second, that there should be an essentially *non-local* description of space–time at the basic level (as would seem to have importance in relation to the space–time non-locality involved in the 'EPR paradox' referred to above). Twistors may, in the first instance, be viewed as entire light rays (photon histories) in space-time. If we take such a light ray to be represented as a single point in another space—which for the moment let us call *twistor space*, a space which we shall try to regard as more primitive than the space–time itself—then, in twistor terms, we can represent a space–time point conversely as the family of light rays that pass through that point, i.e. as a locus in twistor space representing such a family. This locus turns out to be naturally describable as a Riemann sphere, see Fig. 22. (The light rays through a particular space–time event describe the *celestial sphere* as seen by an observer at that event, and it turns out that the Lorentz transformations that one must apply on passing from one observer to another at the same event are identical with those transformations which preserve the complex-curve structure of a Riemann sphere.) The idea is to regard the whole of twistor space as a complex space. For Minkowski's space–time of special relativity, this works remarkably well—although to get the whole of twistor space, we must demand that the light rays represent the space–time histories not of simply massless point particles, but of extended objects that describe the spin and energy of a massless particle like a photon. (An actual photon does indeed spin left-handed or right-handed about its direction of motion.) This is not the place to describe the many subtleties and unexpected mathematical interrelationships that arise in twistor theory. The theory has turned out to have a number of different applications within areas of pure mathematics

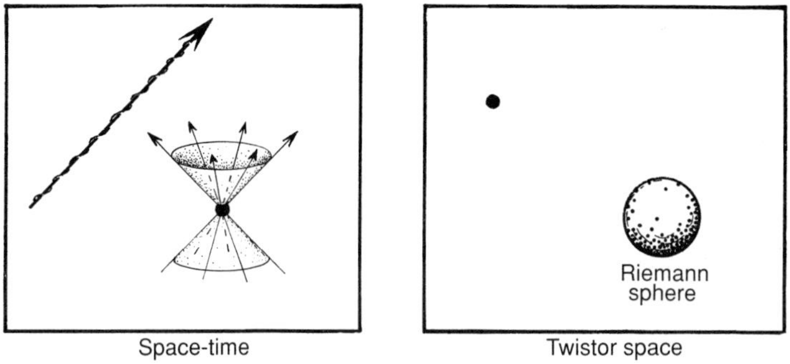

Fig. 22 The twistor correspondence: the space–time history of a (spinning) massless particle (*left*) is represented as a single point in twistor space (*right*); a point in space–time, described in terms of the light rays through it (*left*), is represented as a Riemann sphere in twistor space (*right*).

(mainly differential geometry, representation theory, and integrable systems). The main successes on the physical side have been in general relativity (although a full description of Einstein's equations remains fundamentally elusive) and in quantum field theory. Most significantly, Hodges has found a way of eliminating infinities in QED and electroweak theory, within the context of twistor diagram theory (the twistor analogue of Feynman diagram theory). So far, twistor theory provides only a body of techniques and it is not an independent physical theory. (A scheme due to Singer and Hodges, possibly leading to such a theory, arises if twistor ideas are combined with the ideas of *conformal field theory*—a mathematical theory using the Riemann surfaces from string theory—in higher dimensional form.)

There is no shortage of alternative TENTATIVE schemes (such as other higher-dimensional generalizations of string theory called *membrane* theory) and there is no consensus as to the form that the next SUPERB theory is likely to take, though most theoretical physicists are in agreement that there are indeed further SUPERB theories to be found. The combination of quantum theory with general relativity—the finding of the correct *quantum gravity* theory—is accepted as being one of the profound challenges of such a future theory, although not many physicists yet seem to share my own view that this will entail a fundamental change in the very structure of quantum theory in which **U** and **R** will be united in a single non-linear procedure. If one point of agreement can be found, however, it is the faith—implicit or explicit—underlying all these endeavours: that future successes must come through yet deeper investigations of the interrelations between mathematics and physics. Perhaps *The Modern Physicist's View of Nature* can be summed up as this faith: that there *is* indeed a profound harmony between mathematics and the workings of the natural world!

FURTHER READING

Some of this article is based on ideas described in my semi-popular book (Penrose), where further discussion may be found of some of the SUPERB theories described above. For a very thorough account of the development of physics over the past hundred years, see Pais. For popular accounts of the more recent (including USEFUL and TENTATIVE) theories, see Barrow, Close, Peat, and Squires.

J. D. Barrow, *The world within the world* (Oxford University Press 1988).

F. Close, *The cosmic onion: quarks and the nature of the universe* (Heinemann, London 1983).

A. Pais, *Inward bound* (Oxford University Press, Oxford 1986).

F. D. Peat, *Superstrings and the search for the theory of everything* (Contemporary Books, Chicago, IL 1988).

R. Penrose, *The emperor's new mind: concerning computers, minds, and the laws of physics* (Oxford University Press 1989).

E. Squires *To acknowledge the wonder* (Adam Hilger, Bristol 1985).

6

The modern biologist's view of nature

ROBERT M. MAY
Department of Zoology, University of Oxford

The biologist's view of nature today is, in all essentials, that given by Darwin over a century ago. This view has been summed up by many people in many ways, but as good as any is the recent (and, given the disputatious background to teaching evolution in US schools, pleasing) statement by the California Board of Education: 'evolution is the central organizing theory of biology, and has fundamental importance in other sciences as well. It is not more controversial in scientific circles than gravity or electricity is.'

Basically, ideas about evolution rest on two sets of facts. First, within all plant and animal populations there is noticeable variability, and to some extent these varying properties are inherited. Second—as dramatized by the exhibit in the Smithsonian Museum of Natural History in Washington DC showing a kitchen swarming with all the cockroaches that would result if all the progeny of one female survived to adulthood—natural populations, from cockroaches to elephants, have the intrinsic capability to do more than replace themselves, so that any organism would tend to show runaway population growth were it not held in check, over the long run, by various kinds of mortality. Such mortality, operating on the heritable variation within populations, can result in differential survival, with those genotypes that are better adapted to the physical and biological environment in a particular place at a particular time leaving, on average, more offspring. There may be long periods when survival is essentially random, or when it follows some unchanging pattern, so that the average genetic constitution of the population remains static. But over the long sweep of evolutionary time, in changing environments, such differential survival acting on heritable variation is likely to lead to systematic changes in the genetic constitution of a population, and eventually to the emergence of new species, genera, families—to evolution by natural selection.

The century and more since Darwin has seen accelerating advances in our understanding of the complexities of this process, at every level from molecules to communities of interacting populations. The essential implications for our view of ourselves remain relatively unchanged: no longer the capstone of a universe created for us, we are part of a mechanistic world, sharing with all the other organisms on the planet a common history of evolution by natural processes operating over long times in environments that are themselves changed by evolutionary advances and retreats. We are not unique in using tools, nor in effective communication with each other. We have, however, carried communication and tool-using way beyond any precedent set by other species. As a result, humans have for the past few millennia—and to an accelerating degree over the past few centuries—been able to manipulate natural environments to an extent that has no parallel in the history of life on Earth.

In what follows, I will first mention some unresolved problems that I find interesting, having to do with evolutionary biology and with how we see ourselves. Pre-eminent among these is how many species there are on earth, and why this number rather than more or fewer. I conclude with a view to the future, emphasizing current and likely future rates of extinction of species as a consequence of human activities. My conclusion is that humanity today does indeed have a very special place in nature, not because we were divinely created to use it and rule it, but rather because we have—for what must be a fleeting moment in evolutionary time—cast off the shackles that keep populations in check, and in so doing threaten, by the continuing increase in human numbers and associated activities, to bring about the end of history in the natural world.

SOME CURRENT ISSUES IN EVOLUTIONARY BIOLOGY

The greatest single advance in science in recent times, in my view, is the unlocking of the genetic code in the 1950s. The emerging understanding of the molecular machinery that codes for the assembly of self-replicating organisms makes it possible to ask questions about evolutionary processes at the level of individual molecules. Mutations, by producing novelties, are the raw stuff of evolution; it is now possible to investigate the detailed structure and function of changes in individual sequences of proteins. As more and more is learned about such molecular machinery, I believe it will usher in a biological revolution, every bit as remarkable (and with consequences every bit as unforeseeable) as the earlier industrial/technological revolution, as we learn to produce food, medicines, and other materials by tinkering with the basic genetic machinery that codes for the construction of living things.

An improving understanding of the evolutionary history of particular molecules—of the new 'fossil records' written in the genome—will shed light, amongst other things, on the early origin of the simplest self-replicating organisms on Earth. This, in turn, may help answer a question that many people find uncomfortably vague or 'unscientific': is it likely that ours is the only inhabited planet in the universe, or is life likely to have evolved independently many times, in many different places?

The suggestion that ours may be the only inhabited planet may seem disconcertingly pre-Copernican. But if a clearer understanding were to suggest that the evolution of self-replicating organisms is an extremely unlikely event, then it would not be anthropocentric to suggest our planet is unique; we would be the only ones asking these questions simply because there is not anyone else! So far, the radio-astronomical search for evidence of life elsewhere (the Search for Extra-Terrestrial Intelligence, SETI) has found nothing, which has led some astronomers to suggest we may indeed be unique. The 'garbage-mould argument' suggests that if Earth is not alone, then extraterrestrial life should be abundant (the intuitive argument runs that either your garbage can has no mould, or it is conspicuously mouldy; you are unlikely to find just one or two small specks), and if so we should have evidence by now. Ostriker, at Princeton University, has borrowed from ecological studies of the dynamics of prey-predator systems in patchy environments to argue that, if other inhabited planets carry out into space the kinds of behaviour that have marred human history on Earth, then much of the universe could be empty even though life may commonly originate.

Whatever the merits of these arguments from the wilder shores of science, and whatever the facts of the SETI programme, it will be interesting to see the progress toward a reliable, molecularly based estimate of how likely it is for life (in the sense of self-replicating molecules) to originate. Apart from the fundamental importance of this question, I see even more poignancy in the fears expressed at the end of my chapter if Earth is, indeed, the universe's only inhabited planet.

Until comparatively recently most evolutionary biology has dealt with the reconstruction of phylogenetic relationships, with the way evolution has shaped animal behaviour in response to particular ecological and environmental settings, and with other questions at the level of whole organisms, or populations of them. An emerging understanding of the molecular biology of the gene, however, enables us to make a start on understanding the molecular basis of how cells work, and how early embryonic development unfolds. We can thus begin to comprehend, in a fundamental way, how an organism's evolutionary response to a particular environmental challenge may be constrained by developmental inflexibilities; how evolutionary chance is constrained by developmental and other necessity.

Furthermore, evolution is currently seen primarily as acting on individuals, or at most on groups of relatives (an individual's 'inclusive fitness' is measured by its own reproductive success, plus those of its relatives, each discounted in proportion to the average number of shared genes). But, as Buss of Yale University has emphasized in a stimulating book *The evolution of individuality*, the history of life is essentially a history of the elaboration of new self-replicating entities by the self-replicating entities contained within them. In Buss's words, 'self-replicating molecules created self-replicating complexes, such complexes created (or became incorporated into) cells, cells obtained organelles, and cellular complexes gave rise to multicellular individuals. At each transition —at each stage in the history of life in which a new self-replicating unit arose—the rules regarding the operation of natural selection changed utterly.' Such consideration of the kind of selective forces that would have operated during the early stages of the evolution of multicellular organisms leads to new insights and speculations about developmental trajectories and constraints.

Two areas in particular—immunology and neurobiology—seem to me especially likely to benefit from a combination of current advances ranging from elucidation of molecular mechanisms to growing understanding of 'chaos' and other aspects of the dynamical behaviour of non-linear systems.

As Haldane first emphasized, infectious diseases have probably been the main selective agent acting on human populations at least since the agricultural revolution, some 10 000 years ago, and probably for much longer. One consequence is that the immune system (lymph glands, spleen, antibodies, and lymphocytes, etc.) makes up some 2 per cent of the weight of an adult human. There is an increasingly elaborate taxonomy of the different kinds of cells that constitute the immune system, and of mechanical aspects of how such cells operate in response to an invading virus or other infectious agent. This ensemble of cell-types itself represents a complex multispecies community, whose dynamical properties have only just begun to be investigated. Prominent among the many interesting, but unanswered, questions is what sets the limit to antibody diversity.

The average human has a population of around 10^{20} individual antibodies (of which some 2 per cent die daily and are replaced by 'births' from bone marrow), distributed among roughly 10^8 types. This number, 10^8, is roughly the same for all vertebrates. Much of this diversity is generated within an individual, over the first year or so of life, by gene shuffling during replication, copying errors, and somatic mutations. Each individual thus has his or her own unique complement of antibodies; the total number of possible types is currently unknown. But what mechanisms put a limit to the number of distinct antibody types in any one individual, bringing the somatic generation of diversity to equilibrium after a year or so? Jerne has suggested the explanatory mechanism may be analogous to that which sets limits to the average number of species in communities of interacting populations. In broad terms, the suggestion is that the overall antibody diversity is ultimately regulated by the interactions among antibody species, in much the same way as species diversity in particular environments is ultimately limited by the interactions (competition, mutualism, prey–predator) among the populations. It is often said that one of the difficulties in evolutionary biology is that there is only one world to study. But if Jerne's idea is correct then, for the immune system, each individual is an island-universe, with each body populated by its own unique complement of antibody species that are 'evolved' in infancy. If these notions survive the closer examination they are beginning to receive, they could provide a kind of test-bed for some of the questions about global diversity developed below.

The network of connections among cells in the brain is another instance of a complex dynamical system, that assembles itself afresh in each individual; the general lines are undoubtedly laid down by developmental programmes, but the details seem likely to be somewhat existential. In this sense, the brain may resemble the immune system in being a system of interconnected populations (of neurons rather than antibodies) that 'evolves' in each island-individual, subject to rules set partly by the dynamical behaviour of such complex systems. Current work on the self-organization of 'neural networks', and their ability to store, process, and recover information, seems to me likely to be more relevant to the construction of computers that are particularly efficient for certain classes of activity, than to real understanding of animal brains. But such studies of neural networks represent first steps down a road which I believe will eventually lead not just to an understanding of how evolutionary processes have put together the bits and pieces that add up to the human brain, but also (as for the immune system) to more general insights into the evolution of complex arrays of interacting elements.

HOW MANY SPECIES, AND WHY

To paraphrase Dobzhansky, evolution is the central idea in biology, without which nothing else makes sense. As we have just seen, much progress has been made—over the century and more since Darwin and Wallace—in elucidating the details of how organisms evolve and how new species originate. The ultimate test, however, is to understand what limits the diversity of species in any one particular place and time, and thence, eventually, what limits the overall diversity of life on Earth. Why are there something like 200 species of breeding birds in Britain, rather than 2 or 20 000? Why this number in Britain, but something like 700 in North America? And why a global total of around 9000 species of birds, but 300 000 species of beetles known to science, and possibly many more yet to be catalogued?

Curiously, more progress has been made on the seemingly more complex questions (such as the molecular biology of the genome) than on these basic questions about species numbers. Indeed, we do not even know precisely how many species have been recorded and given Latin binomial names. This number lies somewhere in the range 1.5 to 1.8 million, but no central record has been established and so this simple factual question does not have a crisp answer. It says a lot about human institutions and human values—still anchored in a pre-Darwinian past that sees humans as standing grandly above the rest of the natural world—that we have a comprehensive, computerized catalogue embracing every single book in the Library of Congress, undergirded by money, people, and a robust institutional structure, but no analogous catalogue or undergirding structure for recording the species with which we share the planet.

Even if such a central catalogue of recorded species did exist, it would be grossly incomplete. There are clearly many more species, particularly smaller species, that are yet unknown and unnamed. How many? One estimate runs as follows. Among well-studied groups of larger animals, such as birds and mammals, there are roughly two species in tropical regions for every one in temperate and polar regions. But most currently recorded species are smaller creatures (something like 70 per cent are insects), and of these incompletely studied groups of smaller organisms most are from temperate regions. A conservative estimate is thus that for every named (usually temperate) insect species there are something like two tropical species yet to be recorded, which would give a global total of around 3 to 5 million species. As we shall see below, various kinds of recent work suggest the total may, in fact, be much larger yet.

One approach toward studying species diversity is to ask how many species there are in different categories of physical size. This is obviously one of the first questions Noah must have asked, in producing preliminary design sketches for his ark. For particular groups, such as all mammals, or all birds, or beetles in Britain, or butterflies in Australasia, there are data that suggest a consistent pattern: at larger sizes, for each step down by a factor of ten in characteristic length, there are very roughly 100 additional species; eventually this shades into some lower limit to the characteristic length for organisms in this group, and species numbers fall away rapidly as characteristic lengths decrease below this limit. If one combines all the species of terrestrial organisms—with the species–size relations for some taxonomic groups being necessarily rough estimates—this pattern is repeated on a larger scale. As one moves from characteristic dimensions of metres and more down to a centimetre, from elephants to houseflies, the $(\text{dimension})^{-2}$ rule applies; each factor of ten decrease in characteristic dimension produces a 100-fold increase in species numbers. At dimensions of around one centimetre and below, however, the curve begins to turn over.

Since we have no agreed explanation for the empirical species–size relation itself, this turn-over at small sizes may be real. But, at least for organisms in the size range from around one centimetre to a millimetre and below, it seems more likely that it reflects lack of systematic study of these smaller creatures. Indeed, if the $(\text{dimensions})^{-2}$ rule is projected down to the one millimetre size-classes of terrestrial organisms, we arrive at an estimate of a global total of a few tens of millions of species, most of which are, of course, tiny things that have yet to be recorded. We will return to this estimate below.

Incidently, this species-size scaling relation has implications for Noah's ark, which run contrary to my original intuition. As we run from big things to small ones, each factor of ten decrease in characteristic dimension means 100 times more species, but the constituent individuals each occupy only 1/1000 the volume. Thus, as we move one decade down the size range, the total number of representatives from the species (the animals go in two-by-two) can be squeezed into roughly one tenth the volume! Allowing for problems in packing in little things, a conservative estimate is that the ark requires no more space, and probably less space, for the totality of terrestrial species in the size range one millimetre to one centimetre than for the corresponding organisms in the range ten centimetres to one metre. In short, if you can get all the large vertebrates onto the ark—and there are enough of them to make the ark bigger than the Great Eastern by my reckoning— then the problem is essentially solved. The space requirements do not seem to diverge toward the lower size-ranges, as I would initially have guessed.

In addition to species–size relations, studies of other kinds of empirical patterns help provide a basis for understanding how communities of interacting species are assembled, and thence how diversity is governed. For instance, data on the total numbers of plant-eating insects in different categories of physical size suggest that small creatures actually see a world with more space and more architectural detail. Recent ideas about 'fractal geometry'—rough objects whose surfaces literally have larger and larger areas as you look at them on finer and finer scales (quite unlike the respectable, conventional Euclidean geometrical objects we all met in school) —help explain these observed numbers–size relations. Other investigations document the ways in which individuals are partitioned among species in a community. Such empirical and theoretical studies of the patterns in the relative abundance of species shed light on the underlying causes of commonness and rarity, and on the way communities change in response to particular kinds of disturbance.

Parallel to these patterns in relations among numbers of species, numbers of individuals, and characteristic physical sizes, are a different set of patterns having to do with who eats whom, or who helps or competes with whom. Such interconnections among species end up shaping the structure of entire 'food webs'. Recent years have seen much activity in the assembly of synoptic collections of studies on, for instance, ratios of prey to predators or of plant-eating insects to numbers of plant species. This work culminates in the analysis of a growing collection—currently running around 113—of entire food webs, demonstrating consistent patterns in average numbers of species that a given species interacts directly with (namely, approximately three to five), in the overall average number of links in chains connecting plants through consumers to top predators (typically three to five, for communities in many different environments), and in more detailed aspects of the patterns of interconnection.

One summary finding from such investigations is that, for insects found on temperate-zone plants, there are characteristically around ten species of insects for each species of plant. If this held as a grand generalization, we could go from the currently recorded 300000 species of plants to an estimate—independent of those above—of around 3 million species in total. But, as will be discussed more fully below, work on the arthropod fauna associated with tropical trees suggests the figure may be closer to 100 species of insects and other creatures per species of tropical tree, for a global total of around 30 million.

The work sketched above refers either to patterns in local assemblies of species, or to global totals. Other lines of enquiry focus on the geographical ranges of species, and on the way species totals are related to habitat area (particularly the areas of isolated islands). At one level, such studies begin to quantify what we mean by commonness and rarity. They point the way to teasing apart the different kinds of rarity that exist: locally abundant, but found only in one habitat in one place (the silversword plant in volcano craters in Hawaii); widespread, but in specialized habitat and always sparse; and so on.

At another level, such studies ask how is the number of bird species, or plant species, or insect species related to area among an archipelago of real islands in the ocean, or virtual islands as in freshwater ponds or isolated mountain tops. MacArthur and Wilson's classic work on 'Island Biogeography' showed that very general such species–area relations did indeed exist, and can be summed up by saying that for each decrease by a factor of ten in island area there is a corresponding decrease by a factor or two in the number of species (within a particular group, and therefore more generally). This generalization, which has yet to receive an agreed explanation, is important for its own sake. It also has obvious practical implications for the long-term fate of island reserves that are set aside as a 'part of the main', while the larger region around them is degraded.

Several of these lines of enquiry suggest upward revision in the total number of species on Earth, from the recently conventional estimate of three to five million. But all such suggestions are obviously very speculative. A more concrete basis for such an upward revision is provided by recent work by Erwin (from the Smithsonian Institution) and others. Erwin used insecticidal fog to 'knock down' and collect all the arthropods in the canopies of individual tropical trees; the canopy faunas are inaccessible, and consequently have not received much previous attention. Erwin, who is a beetle specialist, found that typical tree canopies contained around 1000 species of beetles, most of them new to science. To work from this fact to an estimate of global diversity requires that a chain of argument be constructed.

First, how many of this thousand and more species of beetles are specialized to a given tree species, as opposed to being more generally distributed? Making rough assessments of the proportions, separately for herbivorous, predatory, fungivorous, and scavenging beetles, Erwin arrived at a figure of around 160 beetle species specialized on a given tree species (the number derives essentially from the estimate that 20 per cent of herbivorous beetles are specialists). Of recorded insects, 40 per cent are beetles. If this proportion holds in general, then we expect $160/0.4 = 400$ insect species per tropical tree. Again, this is just a best-guess; if essentially all insects are unknown tropical ones, the 40 per cent figure is perhaps irrelevant. The third link in the chain is conservatively to estimate one species elsewhere on the tree for each two insects in the canopy, for a total of 600 insects per tree. Multiplying this number by the estimated global total of 50 000 species of tropical trees, Erwin arrives at an estimate of 30 million insects in total.

Although it is easy to cavil at each step in Erwin's chain of argument, the work is important in providing a new and focused approach to the problem of estimating how many species there are. Erwin does not so much answer the question, as define an agenda of research. Apart from anything else, I believe our ignorance of tropical mites—to name but one group—is at least as great as the ignorance about beetles and other arthropods that Erwin has so dramatically exposed. These other groups may be similarly diverse.

The question of how many species there are is important of itself. I imagine that 'how many species' would be the first question the Starship Enterprise would ask of a newly discovered and inhabited planet (although Star Trek reflects current societal values accurately by never even dealing with what scientific questions are asked of new planets). More significantly, I believe the question stands as a metaphor for how a modern biologist views nature: we seek a fundamental understanding of how evolutionary forces have shaped the diversity we see, rather than much more or much less, yet we do not even know such basic facts as how many species there are.

A VIEW TO THE FUTURE

Lifting our eyes from the local, 'ecological' time scales on which we have been looking at communities, we now turn to view things over the sweep of geological time. Can any lessons be learned from past extinctions, about the characteristics that make for long-term survival of a species? One analysis, by Van Valen of the University of Chicago, suggests that—although average extinction rates vary from group to group—within a given group of organisms past survival is no guarantee of future success. Instead, species' lifetimes within a given group follow a pattern broadly consistent with extinction being likely to happen at any time, irrespective of whether a species has recently originated or has been around for eons. Van Valen's work is often referred to as the Red Queen hypothesis; like the Red Queen in *Alice in Wonderland*, a species has to keep running hard to stay in place. Insofar as there is a degree of exception to this generalization, it seems—not surprisingly—that being very widely distributed helps a species survive, particularly during those episodes of relatively high extinction rates that characterize the conventional boundaries between the geological epochs. Against this background, a very rough generalization may be that approximately half the species present today originated somewhere around 50 to 100 million years ago.

At the beginning of this chapter, I wrote of the intrinsic capacity for any species to more than replace itself from generation to generation. Usually this capacity is restrained by various environmental and biological checks and balances (leading to the possibility for differential survival, whose implications Darwin first realized). Pre-eminent among the still unanswered questions about our own past is how were human numbers maintained roughly constant (with overall rates of population growth being imperceptible) over hundreds of thousands of years, before the advent of the agricultural revolution some 10 000 years or so ago? An increasing amount of evidence suggests the explanation lies not primarily in high death rates among infants and adults, but rather in longer intervals between births than is characteristic of rapidly growing populations today. From the work of Short, Potts, and others, it seems likely that ovulation can be suppressed for intervals of up to three years while infants are being breast-fed at frequent intervals.

Whatever the explanation for the relative stasis before the agricultural revolution, afterwards human numbers launched upon a slowly accelerating increase that has no precedent or parallel in any other biological population. Accelerating again in the wake of the scientific/industrial revolution in the seventeenth and eighteenth centuries, human numbers first reached one billion around 1850, then took another 80 years to double to 2 billion around 1930, and doubled again in 50 years to around 4 billion in 1980. The total is now over 5 billion, with a net addition of approximately 100 million individuals each year (this number represents births less deaths; the number of births is significantly larger). This amounts to a net addition of three people each second, or about 10 000 each hour. These numbers defy any intuitive comprehension.

Associated with this extraordinary explosion in human numbers is understandable and inescapable pressure on natural, semi-managed, and managed ecosystems everywhere. The pressure appears particularly acute in tropical regions, where 1 to 2 per cent of the total area of tropical forest is cleared annually. This is an area roughly the size of the UK. In our understandable focus on the implications of such activity—so vast in scale and swift in time—we tend to forget that Britain killed essentially all its big animals and cut down essentially all its pristine forest so long ago that we sometimes seem to accept the human-created landscape of today (a kinder, gentler landscape?) as if it were the temperate-zone analogue of the tropical rain forest. It is not. And the Mediterranean rim is a desolate memory of what it once was. Our advice to tropical countries would come with greater moral authority if we were doing more to conserve and restore European habitats.

On the other hand, the work of Erwin and others confirms intuitive beliefs that tropical habitats are, hectare for hectare, vastly more diverse than temperate ones ever were, and that tropical species tend to be more specialized in their requirements and more localized in their geographical ranges. So the implications of clearing tropical forests are indeed much more severe than those of clearing corresponding areas of temperate habitat.

Estimates of current extinction rates, essentially all associated with human activities, are uncertain, even for comparatively well-known groups. The *Red data book* of the International Council for Bird Preservation (ICBP) lists 88 bird species as having become extinct since 1600, and 283 as extant but endangered, which constitutes 1 and 3 per cent of bird species respectively. The 88 extinctions have been at an exponentially growing rate, with about half being in this century. The lengthy procedures required for inclusion in the *Red data book*, however, have the consequence that the book was seriously out of date by the time it was published. Moreover, it tended to exclude species from less-studied regions, which often are tropical regions under great pressure. A new ICBP study produced in 1988 listed 1029 bird species at risk of global extinction, and a further 637 species considered significantly threatened. This adds up to around 20 per cent of all species either extinct or at risk.

Diamond, of UCLA, goes beyond this to observe that in the areas he knows best—New Guinea, Melanesia, and Indonesia—some of the species listed as 'threatened' are surely extinct, because they occur on small islands and have not been seen for 50 years by residents of those islands who knew the species well. For these reasons, the ICPB is shifting its emphasis from 'Red Books' of species proven to be extinct toward 'Green Lists' of species proven to be extant and secure. Projecting from his knowledge and experience, Diamond suggests that less than half of the world's roughly 9000 species of birds would qualify for inclusion in such a catalogue of security.

Similar figures pertain to other relatively well-studied groups. For instance, a recent four-year search for the 266 species of freshwater fishes that have been recorded from the Malay Peninsula found only 122—fewer than half—of the species. There is fairly general agreement that these figures are representative (and even conservative, bearing in mind the much greater tendency to extreme endemism for most tropical insects), and that something like half of all terrestrial species are likely to become extinct over the next 50 to 100 years, if current trends persist.

It is sometimes said that, since eventual extinction is the fate of most species, why be concerned about the looming spasm of extinction. This misses the point about relative time scales. For most of the history of life on Earth that is preserved in the fossil record, rates of extinction and rates of speciation have been roughly commensurate. Taking the estimate that roughly half the extant species evolved in the last 50 to 100 million years, along with the estimate that maybe half of all extant species will become extinct in the next 50 to 100 years if current rates of tropical deforestation continue, then contemporary rates of speciation are of order one million times slower than rates of extinction. Were speciation rates plotted as the y-axis on a graph ten centimetres high, then on the same scale extinction rates would require an x-axis extending ten kilometres.

Why should we care if we do extinguish half or more of the other species on our planet? One argument is that they provide a gene bank, an ultimate and irreplaceable source of novelty, for new foodstuffs, medicines, and other products. But maybe we can be clever enough, as our understanding of the molecular machinery of living things deepens, to modify existing crops to serve any new end and to custom design new drugs and vaccines. In the final analysis, I believe we should cherish and conserve diversity primarily for the ethical reason that we now recognize we are no more, though no less, than a part of it; no longer can an educated person see the world as a God-given inheritance to wreak to human ends.

Beyond this, I believe we should be driven to understand the natural world of living things for the same fundamental reasons that we are driven to understand the physics of the unimaginably small and of the unimaginably large. We also need such understanding to manage the biosphere in a sustainable way—which we are not doing at present. Sadly, and in contrast to the search for comprehension of the physical world sketched in the previous chapter, our search for comprehension of the origins of, and the limits to, species diversity takes place against a time limit, with the clock ticking faster as human populations continue to increase.

Index